Shadow Monsters

& Courageous Hearts

STORIES OF RECOVERY TO EMPOWER AND INSPIRE

Hayley has carefully crafted stories that contain the essence of many of the most common emotional problems facing children. They are laced with uplifting moments of humour and playfulness, making them a very enjoyable as well as informative read. Beautiful illustrations are the icing on the cake.
– Hannah Galvin, Child and Adolescent Psychotherapist

The words and illustrations in Shadow Monsters and Courageous Hearts enable the reader to gain an insight into the 'hows and whys' of some common mental health concerns experienced by us all. Hayley Graham has crafted such a beautiful book that exploration of these feelings no longer holds the fear and uncertainty that so often blocks this important emotional learning.
– Jane Andrews, counsellor, trainer and parent

Hayley Graham's book is a terrific contribution to the worlds of child psychotherapy, play therapy and bibliotherapy. She has skilfully and playfully captured the language and sharing of information pitched at parents and carers.
– Di Gammage, Child Psychotherapist, Play Therapist and author of
Playful Awakening – Releasing the Gift of Play in Your Life

These intriguing stories and delightful illustrations will certainly engage the imaginations of child listeners or readers. More importantly, they allow children to think about, and explore, their own thoughts and feelings.
– Patrick Browning, Clinical Hypnotherapist

Shadow Monsters & Courageous Hearts

STORIES OF RECOVERY TO EMPOWER AND INSPIRE

Hayley Graham

Illustrated by Tor Allen

Foreword by Graham Music

Little
Steps
PUBLISHING

Contents

Preface

I fell in love with stories when I was five years old. One of my earliest memories is of waiting for my father in the local library's reception, poring over *The Tales of Beatrix Potter*, transfixed by the beautiful colour plates veiled with sheets of tracing paper.

For me, stories were to become a retreat, an education, and a sign that I wasn't alone in the world. They seemed to speak to me personally and gave me many gifts, including an enduring interest in the human condition. I think it was this, among other things, that drew me to psychotherapy.

The 'among other things' was my own mental health story. I was a solitary, anxious child, and my mother died when I was a teenager. In hindsight, it is unsurprising that I struggled as a young mother, and my children had their ups and downs as a result. In many ways, I was extremely fortunate, but at times, life was tough and help seemed hard to come by. My journey to becoming a therapist began as a mission to understand, heal and find a way forward. It became a drive to do all that I could to help adults and children in a similar position. I now work full time as an adult psychotherapist in a private practice and as a child psychotherapist in schools. I am also the founder and director of the Devon-based charity, BOUNCE! Brighter Futures Foundation, which delivers mental health services to children and families.

So in a way, this book is a distillation of two of my greatest passions. I hope you enjoy it and find it of some help.

– HG

Foreword

I am very pleased to write a brief foreword to this delightful book, one which is informative at many levels, conscious and unconscious. Hayley Graham uses her rich imagination and storytelling gifts to describe emotional worries and issues that both children and parents, as well as educators, will recognise all too well.

Hayley is pushing into new and much-needed territory here in marrying the art of emotionally meaningful storytelling with really helpful synopses and sets of tips for adults to help children and themselves make sense of issues, which are beautifully portrayed in the stories.

Each story evokes, rather than explains, a specific issue in a way that educates without the reader necessarily knowing it. They all stand up as lovely, emotionally nuanced stories in their own right, ones that I think any child and parent would cherish and return to time and again. Each child may find the ones that are most meaningful for them. The book is wonderfully enhanced by the enchanting illustrations which bring to life the themes of each story and the emotional issues evoked.

Almost as a bonus, but a big one, the book has extremely helpful 'top tips' for adults to help us both make sense of big issues – such as trauma, loss and shame, and how they affect children – and to help us talk about these difficult matters with children, all followed up with very helpful information for adults who are interested to pursue things further. I can imagine these sections being extremely helpful for both parents, and also, for example, primary school teachers who want to help but feel uncertain about broaching such topics.

Hayley Graham is a psychotherapist, trainer and also, someone who makes things happen, including developing new and much-needed therapeutic services. She understands how children think and feel, what they need, and also, how to reach them. She also understands what adults need to know to help children. She brings all these gifts together in this wonderful book which I know many parents and children will be really grateful for.

– Graham

Graham Music (PhD) is Consultant Child and Adolescent Psychotherapist at the Tavistock and Portman Clinics, and an adult psychotherapist in private practice. His clinical work has primarily been in working with trauma and exploring the interface between developmental findings. He teaches and supervises nationally and internationally. His publications include: *Respark: Igniting Hope and Joy after Trauma and Depression* (2022); *Nurturing Children: From Trauma to Growth Using Attachment Theory, Psychoanalysis and Neurobiology* (2019); *Nurturing Natures: Attachment and Children's Emotional, Sociocultural and Brain Development* (2016, 2010); *The Good Life: Wellbeing and the New Science of Altruism, Selfishness and Immorality* (2014); and *Affect and Emotion* (2001).

Introduction

Exploring Mental Health Through Stories

Talking about mental health has never been more critical than it is right now – not only our mental health, but our children's, and that of our neighbours, friends and broader communities. Recent research by NHS Digital and The Office of National Statistics shows that mental health difficulties in children and young people rose from one in nine in 2017 to one in six by 2020. Self-harm and thoughts of suicide were also shown to be on the increase. With one in four of us experiencing problems with our mental health in any given year, there's a high chance that we, or someone we know, will be affected.

That's why this book is intended for all young readers, not just those struggling with their mental health. It has three aims. The first is to educate and empower the reader. To give them a greater understanding of mental health difficulties along with the language to talk about them and the confidence to open up and seek help if and when problems arise. The second is to create a kinder, more tolerant and connected world through building awareness and the facilitation of meaningful conversation. The third is to speak directly to young readers already suffering and help them heal.

Given fifty per cent of mental health difficulties manifest by the age of fourteen years old and seventy-five per cent by twenty-four, the sooner we start talking, the better. With this in mind, this book has been written primarily for discussion with young readers of mid-to-late primary ages, although there is no reason it couldn't be used with teens or even adults.

Finding the Tools to Talk

Talking does more than share information. It helps us organise our thoughts, solves problems, reduces stress, brings relief, settles emotions and increases self-esteem. It can grow empathy and build self-compassion. In short, talking can bring about change. It can also prevent tragedies. For me, most importantly, talking can help us form, build and repair relationships.

Knowing where to start when talking about mental health isn't always easy. It is often poorly understood, and much of the available information can be hard to understand and even harder to hold on to. Even with an understanding and the best intentions, launching into a discussion, say about trauma or anxiety, can soon shut down communication rather than open it up.

This book will give you the tools to talk meaningfully about mental health. It is suitable for use by parents, educators, counsellors, psychotherapists and anyone else interested in mental health. The stories provide a simple, effective way of facilitating discussion in group or one-to-one settings.

Stories make it easier for us to understand and retain information. They work for all types of learners and convey complex ideas in engaging and accessible ways that are more likely to influence beliefs and behaviours. More than that, stories provide insight, guidance and help us to make connections. They offer hope and remind us we are not alone, and, as if that's not enough, stories help us find meaning and bring about healing.

If you are a parent reading this book, remember that all children are different. For example, some are emotionally reactive, whilst others are more withdrawn and anxious. There are those who are more sensitive to their environment and can struggle with their mental health at times when others might not. This means that some children are harder to parent than others. The vast majority of the parents I have met are working extremely hard in very difficult circumstances to do the best for their children. All they need is a little support. If you are a parent, be kind to your child … and be kind to yourself.

How to Use This Book

This book is divided into two sections. In Part I, there are five illustrated stories. Each tale is told through the eyes of woodland animals and explores a different aspect of mental health. At the end of each story, you will find a simple explanation and several questions you can use to start a conversation with your child or group. Part II provides more detailed information about the mental health difficulties explored to support you in answering questions and deepen your understanding. It is intended more for the adult reader. You will also find simple suggestions and advice on offering support or getting help.

If you are an adult reading this book, start by reading the illustrated stories, then read through the supporting material in Part II. When sharing the stories with children, they can either be read internally by the child or aloud. The idea is to stimulate curiosity and conversation so the questions can be asked during the story or at the end – whatever works best for you. Sharing the stories isn't intended to be a comprehension exercise. There are no right or wrong answers. It is more a process of exploring thinking, feeling and sensing, in short, a child's personal experience. That said, there is room for some psychoeducation because most children won't have much understanding of what trauma, OCD, shame or attachment are. Whilst the stories can help convey these complex ideas in an easily remembered, engaging, graspable and meaningful way, the background information will support you in answering further questions that might arise and give you what you need to deepen your understanding. Of course, the information provided is limited by its brevity, so the stories are not intended to be an entire course in psychoeducation. It is worth looking at the questions in advance and thinking about your responses and anything else you would like to know. It can also be helpful to share some of your thoughts and experiences to stimulate discussion. Don't feel limited by the questions offered. They're simply suggestions to get things started.

Even though each story is written to explore a specific difficulty, you will find significant overlap. This is true of real life too. You are, for example, likely to find elements of shame in most of the stories, and it can be interesting to view the narratives through different lenses.

At the heart of this book is hope. Hope that it might empower children by giving knowledge and skills to help them navigate the ups and downs of their mental wellbeing as they journey through life, and a wish that it might offer both hope and healing to those that need it most.

PART I
The Stories

ONE
The Courageous Heart

Some years ago …

Exhausted from the chase, the young fox fell at the old wall. With the setting sun tinging the sky red, she looked back over the wispy, yellow grass of the moor. The hunt was not far behind. Catching sight of a small hole within a pile of dislodged stones, she dragged her aching body a few feet more and edged as far back into the darkness as she could.

The bay of the dogs drifted towards her on the cool air. As the pack rose on the horizon, the sound of galloping horses grew to a thunderous roar. Fox froze as they charged down the hill towards her. The horn blared 'gone-to-ground,' and she knew there was nothing more she could do.

As if drowning, she lifted her head and gasped for air. At that moment, a dark shadow arched gracefully overhead, and a voice urged, 'Stay down.' It was the last thing she heard before the scrambling paws and jowls of the hounds.

***

Now …

Fox paced along the edge of the wood, scanning all around and searching as far as she could see, across the expanse of open fields all the way down to the old road that wound its way to the farmer's yard. Owl swept soundlessly across the darkening sky.

'See anything?' Fox called.

'All quiet, bar a few sheep,' Owl laughed. 'Get it? Baaa … a few sheep.'

Fox scowled. 'Easy to joke when you are way up there.'

Owl sighed. Fox was nervous, and when she got nervous, she got snappy. The problem was that Fox was nervous a lot of the time. And nobody knew why, not even Fox.

Owl called back down, 'It's fine, Fox. Nothing for miles.'

Fox shook her head. 'It's too quiet.'

Owl glided down to a nearby tree. She looked quietly at Fox pacing anxiously over the leaves and decided to speak her mind.

'Fox ...'

'What?' Fox said, still scanning the horizon.

'It's too quiet every evening.'

Fox turned and glared at her. 'What do you mean?'

Owl took a breath. 'I mean, maybe it's not the quiet that's the problem?'

Fox's mouth twitched as though she might snarl. 'What are you saying?'

Feeling a pain like the flick of a rubber band on her heart, Owl turned away. She didn't want to make Fox angry.

'Nothing. Nothing at all,' she said. 'How about we stick to the edge of the wood?'

Fox looked up. 'Then we can stay clear of the fallow field?'

Owl nodded. 'And make our way down to the river to see if we can catch a fish or two.'

Fox's eyes glistened. 'That's a good plan, Owl,' she said.

Owl smiled and, with that, flapped her wings and soared into the sky before Fox could change her mind. Crouching, Fox checked left and right, sniffed the air and finally set off.

As time passed and the sun slipped lower, Fox started to feel better. She shook her head and called up to her friend. 'A false alarm after all, Owl.'

Owl swooped low and hovered next to her. 'Better safe than sorry,' she replied.

The pair continued through the twilight in silence, and Fox was soon lost in her thoughts.

Owl soared back into the sky and surfed the air. The river in the valley below came into view and suddenly, a fish jumped. Screeching, Owl swept towards it.

Fox froze at the sound, her heart lurching into her throat.

Owl realised her mistake. 'It's just a fish,' she called.

But then a dog barked, and a horn blew. The fish forgotten, Owl flew towards her friend.

'It's just old Shep,' she called, 'and the farmer in his truck.'

But it was too late. Fox had turned on her heels and run, bolting as if for her life. Owl flew after her, calling out. But Fox wasn't listening – it was like she wasn't even there at all. She ran back and forth, round and round, eyes darting left and right, until BAM! ... she ran headlong into Badger.

The impact knocked them both to the ground. Fox lay panting, and Owl swooped in.

'It's okay, Fox,' she said. 'Old Shep was barking, and the farmer

was tooting his horn.'

'What?' Fox said, sounding dazed.

'The dog … it was old Shep,' Owl repeated, helping Badger to his feet.

Good-natured Badger chuckled quietly. 'Can't say I was expecting that. You okay, Fox?'

Fox groaned. 'What happened?'

Owl explained about the dog and the horn and how frightened Fox had been before saying a little more about sunsets and grass.

Badger listened carefully, and Fox sighed a big sigh. She looked down at the ground, and her shoulders slumped.

'I'm sorry. I know it doesn't make any sense.'

Owl spoke softly. 'It does make some sort of sense, Fox. It's when the sun sets, or when we walk through the long grass of the fallow field or a dog barks.' She paused. 'Maybe something happened, maybe a dog ...'

'No,' Fox said sharply. 'There's nothing. Nothing at all.'

Owl spoke softly. 'At least, nothing you remember,' she said.

Hearing her friend's kindness, Fox's chest heaved, and she gulped back her tears. She looked at Owl and Badger with red-rimmed eyes and waggled her head from side to side.

'Argh,' Fox joked awkwardly. 'Save me from the scary sunset.'

Owl and Badger laughed. Badger dusted bits of grass and mud from his fur and said, 'I think you should speak to Hare.'

The next day, they found Hare lolloping among the bluebells in the dappled afternoon sunlight. She listened carefully as Fox, Owl and Badger told her all about the sunsets and grass and the dog and the horn.

Then Hare pulled at a tuft of grass and munched slowly, her head tilted a little to one side as if thinking. Her eyes opened wider. She turned to look straight at Fox, and her mouth dropped open.

'Quick,' she said, 'there's no time to waste,' and she began to run.

Fox followed close on her heels, and Hare called back, 'Not bad for a fox.'

Badger was left far behind, wheezing a little as he trundled after them.

Hare bounded on through the thick wood until she came to a clearing. She stopped and nodded into the distance.

'There,' she said.

Fox followed her line of sight. At first, she couldn't see anything, but as she searched the landscape, a figure emerged. Sitting regally amidst the tall grass and the russet earth was a stag.

Fox glanced at Hare and checked the sky to see Owl still circling above. Hare hopped forwards, one bound at a time. When she was close enough, she called out gently.

'Stag?'

Stag turned. His muzzle was grey with great age, and he looked tired, but there was something else too ... *sadness*, Fox

thought. Nonetheless, Stag smiled warmly when he saw Hare.

'Hello, Hare,' he replied.

'How are you, Stag?' Hare asked, hopping forwards and rubbing her head against his velvety nose.

'Could be worse,' Stag said.

Fox noticed his breathing was heavy. Owl swept down and settled in a nearby tree.

'I've brought some visitors,' Hare said. 'I thought you could tell them your story.'

Stag chuckled. 'Now, why would a couple of youngsters want

to hear the stories of an ancient stag like me, Hare?'

'Please,' Fox said, a strange sense of familiarity giving her the confidence to speak.

Stag looked at her. 'You really want to know?'

Fox nodded.

'Well, you'd better make yourself comfortable then,' he said softly.

Fox sat as Owl fluttered a little closer.

'It may seem hard to imagine now,' Stag began, looking at Fox, 'but –'

'I'm here, I'm here,' Badger called, blundering into the clearing. 'Did I miss anything?' he said, reaching out to lean against the trunk of a tree, puffing and panting.

Stag laughed out loud.

'Welcome, Badger,' he called. 'You're just in time.'

The four friends made themselves comfortable, and Stag began again.

'It may seem hard to imagine but not so long ago, I was fit and strong – the strongest, some say – and the moor was my home.'

He paused and his eyes took on a faraway look as if he had drifted into the past.

'I remember it was autumn, a glorious day, and I was quite content.' He looked back at the friends. 'You have to understand I'd already lived a good life by then, a long life.' The friends nodded as if they understood. 'I'd been grazing in a copse, and it was getting late. I remember the sky, how beautiful it was, still tinged with the fire of the sun.'

Stag fell silent, and the friends sat, hanging on his every word.

His voice was deep and slow when he spoke again. 'I heard the dogs first. I was about to turn tail and run when I glanced across the wispy, yellow grass of the moor to see a fox. Half your size,' he said, nodding at Fox. He looked away, and his eyes glistened as he shook his head and smiled. 'That fox. The tiniest creature, but my goodness, she ran with the heart of a stag.'

Fox gulped as she felt emotion surge through her body.

'The dogs weren't far behind. I don't know how long she had been running. A long time, I imagine. She fell at the old stone wall but even then, she didn't give up. I watched as she dragged herself into a small hole, using every last ounce of her energy … and that's when I knew I couldn't leave her.'

Tears welled in Stag's eyes, and he took a deep breath. Fox's heart began to pound, and the fur on the back of her neck stood up as images began to flood her mind.

'I knew the dogs would find her, but I reckoned I could throw them off the scent and figured I still had one good run left in me. So, I galloped out onto the moor as the horn was blowing and charged full pelt towards the wall. I leapt with all my might and shouted –'

Fox gasped. 'Stay down,' she blurted out. 'You shouted, "Stay down."'

Stag took a sharp breath and turned to look straight at her, staring in open-mouthed disbelief.

'It was you?'

'It was me, Stag,' Fox said, her eyes filling with tears. 'I remember it now.'

'And you were unhurt?'

'Thanks to you,' Fox said. 'All I could remember for a long time was waking up in a panic and running. As if I'd woken from a nightmare.'

'I went back the next day,' Stag said, 'to see, you know, but I could never be sure …' He stopped again. 'And here you are, safe. You're safe,' he said, his deep voice breaking a little.

Fox let the words drift across her, then she nodded.

'Yes, I am. I'm safe,' she said. She said it again, 'I'm safe,' and then began to laugh. She *was* safe! She skipped and leapt and laughed with joy and the other animals laughed with her.

They shared stories late into the night, becoming the best and firmest of friends. Strangely, Fox didn't even notice the setting sun or the sky tinged with red.

From then on, things improved quite a lot for Fox. She still got frightened sometimes, but now she understood why. So, little by little, with the help of Hare, Badger, Owl and Stag, things

bothered her less and less and what had happened remained in the past, exactly where it belonged.

A Story About Trauma

Fox has trauma.

Have you heard about trauma? What do you know?

When something frightening or upsetting happens to us, or we know of or see it happening to somebody else, especially someone we care about, it can cause trauma. There are no set rules about what causes trauma. What might cause trauma for one person might not cause it for another, so it is important not to judge yourself or anyone else.

What happened to Fox to cause her trauma? Why do you think Stag didn't get trauma?

We are more likely to get trauma when we feel trapped, or when we can't fight or run away. Both Fox and Stag were chased by the hounds, but Fox was trapped, she was too tired to run any further and too small to fight.

When we have trauma, we get big feelings that can be very hard to control, and this can cause problems – perhaps at home with our family or at school with teachers and friends.

What sort of feelings was Fox struggling to control? Who was it causing problems with?

Like Fox, people with trauma often feel very scared or worried. They might get angry or very upset without there seeming to be a good reason for it. They might also be very quiet and withdrawn. They might spend a lot of time in bed or not want to get up and go to work or school. People with trauma often talk about feeling depressed.

Owl cares about Fox but being her friend isn't always easy. Fox gets angry with her and can say hurtful things.

What do you think it would be like to have a friend who was often angry or scared? What do you think you might do in that situation? Do you know what 'depressed' means?

We all have days when we feel a bit fed up. But when we feel unhappy and bad about ourselves most of the time, when we don't want to do anything and feel like we have no energy, we might say we are depressed. Fox feels unhappy and bad about herself. She knows she gets angry and panicky, and she also knows she can be hurtful to Owl but she doesn't understand why.

Sometimes people might not have a clear memory of what caused the trauma, so they do not always know when something reminds them of the trauma and makes them feel frightened, panicky, angry or upset. Fox couldn't remember what happened.

Can you see why Fox felt worried when the sun was setting, the dog barked or the horn blew?

We can find it hard to remember what's happened when we get very frightened or angry because we are using what is known as our survival brain. When we use our survival brain, our thinking and memory brain gets sleepy, so we find it hard to think clearly or recall events. Fox couldn't remember her trauma. When she was being hunted, the sun was setting, dogs were barking and a horn was blown. Now when she is with Owl, without knowing why, she feels anxious when the sun is setting, and when Shep barks and the farmer blows his horn, she panics and runs.

When we have trauma, we get stuck in our survival brain, which can only do a few things – fight, run, freeze or play dead.

Have you ever noticed yourself wanting to fight, run or freeze when you felt scared? What was it like?

When Stag tells Fox his story, she remembers everything that happened. Knowing the whole story helps Fox to overcome her trauma.

What do you imagine it was like for Fox to suddenly remember everything? Were you surprised that she couldn't remember such a terrifying thing? What else do you think helped Fox to overcome her trauma? How could you help someone who has trauma?

Owl and the other animals helped Fox overcome her trauma. We can help people with trauma by helping them to feel safe. There are lots of ways we can do this. We can help them feel safe by doing things that are fun, listening to them talk, or doing things that are calming, such as going for a walk or drawing.

Go to page 109 to learn more and find some simple practices that can help.

Two
The Shadow Monster

Mouse opened the door a crack and peeked into the unlit room. He knew the creature was there. It lurked in the darkest corners, sitting still as stone. Hardly daring to breathe, he waited. Something slithered nearby. Heart thumping, unable to move, Mouse gasped as it loomed out of the blackness. As it lunged towards him, baring its terrible teeth, Mouse found a sudden burst of energy and hurled himself back from the room, slamming the door shut.

Breathless and shaking, he lay back against the door and slid slowly to the floor. There was no longer any doubt in his mind … it was getting bigger.

Sighing, Mouse pulled himself to his feet. As much as his body ached for sleep, Mouse knew what he had to do. He would begin by checking the stones in the old wall. Once he was sure there were no cracks or loose mortar, he would ensure the locks were secure and then inspect the boards over the windows. There was no other way.

Heart beating almost as hard and fast as before, he got to work. Screwing up his eyes to see in the shadows, he worked methodically from top to bottom and left to right.

'One, two, check the edges. Three, four, fill every hole.'

Mouse made his way through each and every stone, paying such close attention to the minutest detail that he forgot all about time. In fact, he forgot about everything.

'Hello?'

Mouse jolted at the sound of the voice. It was Badger … it was always Badger. He called every single day. Mouse shook his head and went back to inspecting the wall, concentrating through gritted teeth.

'Mouse?' Badger called again.

Losing his place for a second time, Mouse kicked the wall and, clenching his fists, stormed towards the front door. *Stupid Badger and his ridiculous questions!* Mouse was going to tell him EXACTLY how he was feeling! As he rounded the corner into the hall, he stopped. There was Badger, his kind face full of worry as he peered in.

Mouse stepped back into the shadows and looked down at his feet, the weight of shame so heavy in his stomach he feared it would drag him deep into the cold ground. A voice in his head was telling him he must be a very bad mouse and that no one, not even Badger, could ever know.

After a minute of waiting and receiving only silence in return, Badger called out that he would come again tomorrow and Mouse watched him leave. Then, with his heart aching and his head bowed, he returned to checking the wall.

The days came, and they went. Badger continued to call on Mouse, and Mouse continued to ignore Badger. Mouse checked every stone again and again. The more he checked, the more fearful he felt. As sleepless day followed sleepless night, he became weak with exhaustion, and as he grew weaker, the creature in the dark room grew stronger.

Yet still, no matter how strong the creature became, no matter how easily it could have overpowered him, every evening, Mouse opened the door and peered into the gloom. He knew he shouldn't, but he had to see if it was still there.

So one evening, like every evening, Mouse quietly and carefully prised open the door and, barely breathing, peered into the darkness. Without warning came a hiss and a howl as the flash of jaws bore down on him. Mouse gasped, screwed his eyes shut and braced himself for its piercing bite.

Just then, there was a knock at the door.

'Hello,' Badger called.

Mouse cried out and, as quick as it had come, the creature was gone. Mouse jumped out of the room, slammed the door and raced to Badger, and this time, he didn't stop. He ran and ran and leapt into Badger's arms.

'Hello, Mouse,' Badger said in surprise.

Hearing the tenderness in his voice, Mouse began to sob and in the gasps between, he told Badger all about the creature in the dark room.

As Mouse spoke and the tears ran down his whiskers and dropped onto Badger's fur, Badger looked at him with kind, thoughtful eyes and said, 'Shall we walk?'

Mouse nodded. Badger gently hoisted Mouse onto his broad shoulders and, as they walked and the sun slipped slowly from

the sky, Mouse's tears began to subside.

As Mouse fell silent, Badger began to talk about the wood, telling Mouse tales of his forest friends. Badger's velvety voice wrapped around Mouse like a soft, warm blanket and, nestling deeper into a bed of his wiry fur, Mouse closed his eyes.

When he opened them, he was curled up on a bed of leaves, and the forest was bathed in moonlight. Badger was sitting next to him, looking up at the night sky. Yawning, Mouse sat up and, for a while, he too looked up at the stars, the thoughts of the creature that had been keeping him from sleep still fresh in his mind.

'I found it in the hedgerow,' he said. The words seemed to burst into the silence.

Badger nodded like he understood, and Mouse continued, lowering his voice a little.

'It was an ordinary day, like any other day,' he said. 'I was picking blackberries and thinking about how cold the winter would be and how I didn't have enough food and how hungry I might be.' He gulped. 'And how hungry the weasels would be … when suddenly, there it was among the brambles. I knew it was dangerous the second I saw it. I tried to run, but it was too fast for me.' He hung his head and sighed. 'It followed me all the way home.'

'What a shock that must have been, Mouse,' Badger said. 'How did you know it was dangerous?'

Mouse thought. 'I know something dangerous when I see it, Badger.'

'It must have looked terrifying,' Badger said. 'So, what

happened next?'

'It followed me everywhere. When I looked around, there it was.' Mouse was talking faster now. 'So, I got a big stick and tried to push it away, but the more I pushed, the stronger it seemed to get. No matter what I did, it wouldn't leave me alone.'

'So, you locked it up?' Badger said.

Mouse gulped. 'I started to worry what the other animals would think and what it might do to them ...' He trailed off and sighed a big sigh.

Badger nodded as if thinking carefully and then stretched, yawned and looked at Mouse a little bleary-eyed.

'And once you'd locked it up, you had to make sure it couldn't escape,' he said.

'Yes,' Mouse said.

Badger lumbered slowly to his feet and looked up at the moon. Mouse followed Badger's gaze.

'It's beautiful,' Mouse said.

The moonlight streamed through the trees. The shadows of the branches seemed to dance on the ground to the rhythmic breath of the air.

Suddenly, Mouse squealed and clasped his paw over his mouth.

'What is it?' Badger said with concern.

Mouse pointed into the dense wood and stammered, 'B-b-bear!'

Badger followed the direction of Mouse's trembling paw, squinting a little as he searched the landscape, trying to see what he could see. A gentle smile spread across Badger's face, and he turned back to Mouse.

'I see it,' he said kindly, carefully scooping up the wide-eyed Mouse and putting him back on his shoulder. 'That does look like one scary bear. Shall we go and say hello?' he said.

Mouse gasped and looked at Badger, ready to object. But seeing that the older animal was unconcerned and realising he felt safe beside him, he nodded, somewhat to his own surprise.

As they walked towards the frightening beast, Mouse watched open-mouthed as, little by little, it began to dissolve, becoming a tumble of branches and shadows.

He sat up tall and exclaimed, 'It wasn't a scary bear at all.'

'No,' Badger said. 'But it was a scary thought.'

Mouse looked at Badger, and they smiled.

'Look,' Badger said, nodding at the ground, stretching himself up tall, so he was standing on his tiptoes with his arms curved above like the branches of a tree.

Mouse laughed and shouted, 'Shadow monster!'

Badger chuckled. 'You know the good thing about shadow monsters, Mouse?'

'No?' he said.

'They never survive the light.'

'Or Badgers,' Mouse laughed.

Badger nodded. 'You know, Mouse. I'd like to meet this creature of yours. What do you say?'

Although Mouse was frightened, he knew somewhere deep in his heart he wanted Badger to meet the creature too, so he said yes.

'Good,' Badger said firmly and started to whistle a cheerful tune as they began the journey home.

As soon as his little house came into sight, Mouse knew the creature was still there. He could feel it, like he could feel the breath of the icy wind on his neck. Badger stopped whistling as if he could feel it too, and they walked the remaining distance in silence.

When they got inside, Mouse climbed down from Badger's shoulder and, with his friend close on his heels, tiptoed to the creature's lair. He hesitated at the door, glancing up at Badger before ever so carefully, ever so quietly, easing it open.

For a moment, they stood together on the threshold. Badger opened his mouth to speak when a gust of wind seemed to come out of nowhere, took the door and slammed it shut. Mouse froze. He held his breath, waiting for the flash of teeth, the swish of a tail. It was then he heard it.

The sound came in waves. A slow *whoosh, whoosh* like the wings of a giant goose in flight. Each wave brought a burst of air that almost swept Mouse off his feet. Holding on to the wall, he strained his eyes against the darkness and, little by little, began to see. The creature seemed to be sleeping, its body pulsing as it breathed.

Badger stepped calmly into the room. Mouse followed, reaching up to take Badger's paw. Together, they moved towards the creature, one step at a time.

As they got closer, its bellowing breath became shallower and when they came to stand beside it, it began to stir. As Mouse tightened his grip on Badger's paw, the creature lazily opened a blood-red eye and Mouse gasped, his heart pounding in his mouth.

'Hello, creature,' Badger said.

In a flash, the creature reared and roared as it stretched wide its terrible jaws. With a hiss, it bore down on them, its cold breath ruffling their fur. Without a thought, Mouse dropped Badger's paw and leapt into the creature's mouth, stretching up tall, straining against its deadly bite as its sharp teeth scratched and pierced his skin.

The creature tossed its head, squealing as it shook Mouse free. With its tail swishing and its body writhing, it bounced off the walls. Mouse picked himself up off the floor. His whole body shook, not with fear but rage.

Pulling himself up tall, he shouted, 'Get out!' and pointed at the door.

The creature snapped and snarled. Mouse held its eye and as it came towards him, he grabbed its thorny tail and swung it with all his might. The creature screeched and scraped with its claws. The more it flailed, the more Mouse fought. Then, in a moment, it was over. The creature went limp. Mouse drew a deep breath and roared as it began to fall, and as it fell, the light of the moon appeared. With the room bathed in its luminous rays, Mouse watched open-mouthed as the creature collapsed to the ground, becoming nothing more than a heap of swirling, moonlit brambles ... brambles that had grown through a hole in the wall.

Mouse gasped and dropped to the floor. He buried his head in his paws, and his body began to shake. Badger came to sit beside

him and gently took hold of his paws, expecting to uncover his tears. But Mouse wasn't crying … he was laughing.

He laughed and laughed and between each laugh, he stuttered, 'It was … it was … just a … ha ha! A pile of brambles?'

'It was,' Badger said. His eyes twinkled as he smiled, but he didn't laugh.

'Ha ha! Just … like the shadow bear?' Mouse chortled, growing calmer.

Badger furrowed his brow and became serious.

'Not quite, Mouse,' he said. 'This time it wasn't enough just to walk up to it and face it. This time you had to leap into its jaws.'

Badger paused. 'That took a lot of courage, Mouse. You couldn't be sure.'

Mouse looked up. 'I couldn't,' he said, his lip beginning to tremble. He took a deep breath. 'But somewhere in my heart, I knew you were, Badger.'

'Do you know why I was sure, Mouse?'

Mouse shook his head.

'Why I never doubted you?'

As tears welled in his eyes, Mouse shook his head again.

Badger smiled and squeezed his paw. 'Because Mouse … I

know you are a *good* mouse.'

Mouse's tears began to fall, he buried his head in his paws again and this time, he cried.

Badger stayed quietly beside him and, after a good while, Mouse looked up and wiped his eyes. He stared at the beams of moonlight streaming in through the hole and casting shadows on the wall. Then he glanced down at the pile of long, jagged brambles which had swished and swiped in the wind and now lay motionless on the floor.

Finally, he chuckled and said, 'It's strange, isn't it, Badger? How a scary thought can seem like it's so much more.'

Badger agreed.

Mouse stretched and yawned. Tomorrow they would have a bonfire and burn those brambles. Smiling as he thought of the two of them working together, he lay back against Badger's wiry coat, closed his eyes and at long, long last, he slept.

A Story About Anxiety and OCD

Mouse struggles with anxiety or worry. This type of intense, constant worrying is known as OCD (Obsessive Compulsive Disorder).

Have you ever heard of OCD? What do you know about it?

It is normal to feel anxious from time to time. Many people worry about having to take a test or perhaps learning to ride a bicycle. In small amounts, worry can be helpful as it might make you work a little harder for your test or be a bit more careful on your bicycle. It can also help focus your attention. Some people think of this sort of 'good worry' as pressure.

Like Mouse, the problem starts when we worry too much. Too much worry might mean you avoid taking the test, or your mind goes blank when you do, or you never learn to ride your bike. When you worry too much, you might imagine the worst possible thing happening, such as 'If I fall off my bike, I'll die,' or 'If one thing goes wrong, everything will go wrong.'

What is the 'worst possible thing' that Mouse worried about? Can you see the difference between Mouse's worry compared to worrying about falling off your bike or taking a test?

Mouse is worried about a shadowy creature attacking and maybe even killing his friends and neighbours. Falling off a bike or taking a test are common, real-life concerns. OCD worries are slightly different and less common. Some people might say these sorts of worries are 'unrealistic'. The creature seems real to Mouse, but shadowy monsters that appear from nowhere are not part of everyday life. In fact, it would be reasonable to think the creature isn't real at all.

To begin with, did you think the creature was real or imagined? How can we tell if a worry is 'real' or not? Is it the worry that isn't real or the thought behind it? Why do you think the creature got bigger in the story?

Our brains are thought-making machines. This is helpful in many ways because it can help us solve problems. Say you need money to buy a new game. You might think, 'I could save my birthday money, I could do some extra chores for extra pocket money, or I could rob a bank.' As you can probably see, some of the thoughts are helpful. Others are just nonsense!

Those who struggle with OCD are bothered by these sorts of random thoughts. They see them as important and do things to cope with the feelings they produce. In the example above, you might start to think you're a bad person for thinking about robbing a bank. You might worry that you will do something 'bad' and get in trouble with the police. To cope with the fear, you might stop going out in case you do something bad.

In the story, the creature is a metaphor for a random thought that pops up in Mouse's head and causes him to worry. Mouse sees it as dangerous. His worry is real but the creature itself isn't. OCD can make it difficult to assess what is real and what isn't real – a little like you might have found it hard to decide if the creature in the story is real or not. In the story, the more Mouse checks on the creature, the bigger it gets. This is because when we have these types of random, unrealistic thoughts, the more things we do to try and stop them or cope with the feelings they produce, the bigger they get.

What does Mouse do to try and cope with the worry?

With OCD, the worry could be about almost anything, and there are as many different ways of coping with the feelings. Here are a few common ones:

Worrying germs might make you sick might mean you wash your hands all the time.

Worrying something bad might happen might mean you touch or tap things like door frames in a particular order.

Worrying you might have hurt someone or done something wrong might mean you go over and over memories in your head, trying to remember if you did anything wrong.

To try and cope with the worry, Mouse spends all his time checking to make sure the creature can't escape. He checks the locks are fastened and the stones in the wall are secure. He does this over and over and doesn't sleep or rest – but the anxious checking still doesn't make the creature go away.

Why do you think the creature vanished when Mouse jumped into its jaws?

To overcome OCD, fears have to be faced. This takes a lot of courage. For example, if someone thinks that they might have germs on their hands that could make them or their family sick, it will be hard for them not to keep washing their hands. They will need to be very brave. When Mouse finally finds the courage to face his fear by leaping into the creature's jaws, he sees it for what it really is: a pile of brambles that had grown through a hole in the wall.

How did Badger help Mouse in the story?

People with OCD often believe their thoughts make them bad. They feel very responsible and fear that something terrible might happen either because of something they do or don't do. Mouse worried that he was 'a bad mouse'. Badger helps Mouse understand he is a good mouse, and he helps him face his fears.

What do you think Badger meant when he said shadow monsters never 'survive the light'?

It is important for people with OCD to share their fears with someone they trust. Keeping worries locked up on the inside only makes them worse.

Go to page 115 to learn more and find some simple practices that can help.

THREE
Finding Someone There

The young squirrel scuttled through the thick carpet of crimson leaves on the forest floor. Pigeon looked down from his perch in the trees above and cooed a friendly hello. He waited patiently for Squirrel to reply, but Squirrel didn't look up. He didn't even stop.

So Pigeon cooed again, louder this time. Squirrel darted from tree to tree, twitching his bushy tail. Occasionally he stopped to sniff the musky earth and dig, but still, he didn't look up. Pigeon puffed out his chest and tried one last time. As his call rang out loud and clear across the wood, he fixed Squirrel with his beady eye and waited once more … but nothing, nothing at all.

Pigeon ruffled his feathers. *Well, I never, in all my days.* He flapped his wings and as he launched himself into the air, he called out, 'Rude!'

Squirrel did his best to pretend he hadn't heard it, like he'd done his best to pretend Pigeon hadn't been there. He clenched his fists, put his head down, and resolved to search faster. In fact, such was the frenzy of his activity, he didn't even notice the old hare. So when he finally caught sight of her, he squealed with fright and jumped straight to the sky. He landed with his eyes wide open and his heart pounding – such was the shock of finding her there.

'Hello,' said Hare.

Squirrel blinked as he looked at her. He thought she had kind eyes but found it hard to be sure.

'I'm sorry I startled you,' she added.

Not knowing what to say, Squirrel looked down and scuffed the earth with his foot.

Hare hopped closer. 'What are you looking for?'

Squirrel took a few steps back. 'Something,' he said.

'I see.' Hare nodded like she understood and lifted a powerful hind leg to scratch her crooked ear. 'Something you've lost?' she asked.

Squirrel thought for a moment. 'Suppose so,' he said with a shrug.

'Hmm,' Hare said. 'Do you know where you lost it?'

Squirrel shook his head, thinking it was a stupid question but not daring to say.

Hare furrowed her brow and narrowed her eyes a little, as if concentrating. Then, she thumped the ground with her foot.

'Ha! If you knew where you'd lost it, you'd know where to find it. Silly old Hare.' Eyes twinkling, she smiled at Squirrel. Thinking she was a little odd but not in a bad way, Squirrel moved closer.

Hare cocked her head to one side. 'Do you know how you lost it?'

'No, sorry,' Squirrel said, feeling perplexed.

'Or why you lost it?' said Hare.

'No.'

Squirrel took a step back, thinking, *What on earth does she mean by 'why'?*

'Or when?' Hare asked.

'No!' Squirrel yelled.

He glared at her, but only for a moment. His eyes widened, and his heart began to pound. Then, his tail twitched, and he turned and ran.

Hare lolloped after him and called out, 'Squirrel ... no wonder you were angry.'

Squirrel stopped and glanced back, his heart still beating fast. Hare smiled, and Squirrel turned to face her, afraid to stay yet not wanting to go.

'I ask too many questions,' Hare said.

Squirrel took a breath, feeling something like the stillness of straight-down summer rain.

'Far too many,' he said and Hare laughed a gentle laugh. There was a moment of quiet: a strange, slightly confusing, but good kind of quiet.

Squirrel hopped a little further forward. 'It was winter, I think. A long, cold winter,' he said.

'That must have been hard.'

Squirrel shrugged. 'I got used to it.'

'Or you found a way through it.'

Squirrel let the words sink in, then he looked up at Hare open-mouthed. 'I think that's how I lost it.'

'When you were finding a way?'

'Yes.'

Hare nodded slowly. 'You know, Squirrel, I think you might be right,' she said. 'Shall I help you look?'

'Okay,' Squirrel said and with that, he began to rifle through the leaves again.

Hare watched him for a moment, feeling a warm tenderness in her heart. Then, she sat back and took a moment to survey their surroundings. 'Tell me what you do remember.'

'It was a bit like the sun,' Squirrel said, without thinking.

'Yellow, then?'

Squirrel chuckled. 'No, it felt warm.' He thought for a moment. 'But on the inside, like a belly full of plump plums eaten on a hot summer's day.'

Hare hopped over to a large fallen branch, lifted it with both paws and peered underneath. 'What does it feel like on the inside now?'

Squirrel stopped searching for a moment, then shrugged again. 'A bit like nothing.'

'Like something is missing?'

'Yes,' Squirrel said.

There was another long pause. Hare strolled around, craning her neck to look behind rocks and standing on her tiptoes to

peer into the low-hanging branches.

Already, the light was getting low, and Squirrel seemed to have lost his bounce.

Hare smiled a gentle smile and said, 'Shall we look again tomorrow?'

Squirrel smiled back. And so, the journey began.

Hare and Squirrel met day after day. Week after week. They searched high and low. Together they crossed snow-covered mountains where they found nothing but the lonely howls of a long-forgotten wind. They endured storms they feared would

break the world apart. They fought and befriended creatures with deadly talons and mighty wings that threatened to blot out the sun. They shared stories and danced with tribes of strangers on soft, golden sands beside calm, blue seas. Sometimes, they laughed, sometimes, they argued, but no matter what happened, Hare noticed that Squirrel never cried.

After many days, they came to a dark wood. A barren, long-forgotten place where a chill wind blew. Squirrel shivered as he looked around at the withered limbs of the blackened trees that stretched as far as he could see.

'Do we need to go in?' Squirrel asked, already knowing the answer in his heart.

Hare replied that it was the only way, so together they stepped into the darkness. They managed to find a path of sorts. A small track that twisted and turned, leading them deeper and deeper into the lifeless wood. Little by little, the path widened. Up ahead, a clearing began to emerge and at its centre, the gnarled trunk of a gigantic, decaying oak.

Suddenly, Squirrel came to a halt, took a sharp breath and said, 'I've been here before.'

The two friends looked at each other, both understanding

that this meant something but unsure what. Squirrel took small steps at first, then, as his confidence grew, he started to run. Hare ran too, staying by his side.

As they reached the tree, Squirrel looked round, his eyes shining with excitement as he raised his arms towards the sky, inviting Hare to look up.

'Do you see how tall it is? Once, you must have been able to climb to the clouds and –'

Squirrel stopped and dropped his arms before scuttling around the tree. 'There was … yes! See, a door here,' he said, his voice becoming muffled as he stepped inside the cavernous tree trunk. Hare followed.

'Then, through here,' Squirrel called, beckoning Hare to follow.

Together they pushed further and further on, the passageway becoming narrower and narrower.

'Nearly there,' said Squirrel.

Hare stooped low, but as the passageway became smaller (smaller than any burrow she'd ever been in before), she began to crawl. Just as Hare thought they could go no further, they came to a dimly lit, empty chamber and could see the hollow trunk of the great oak soaring above them. Rays of light filtered through small holes, shining like stars.

Squirrel looked at Hare and smiled. 'This is the place,' he said.

'What place?'

'Where I lived.'

Hare felt a pang of pain in her heart as she looked around the empty room. 'It was safe here?'

'Yes,' Squirrel smiled as he walked, running his paw across the wooden walls.

'What were you hiding from?'

'Everything,' Squirrel said with a faraway look. 'At times, the snow was this deep,' he said, standing on his tiptoes and stretching his arms above his head, bending his fingers like he was hanging from a wall. His eyes widened. 'And the stoats ...'

Hare waited for Squirrel to continue.

'... were so hungry,' Squirrel went on, standing as still as stone.

'That sounds terrifying,' Hare said.

Squirrel began to breathe deeply. 'It was.'

Hare looked at the empty chamber.

'You did well, Squirrel, to find this place.' She paused for a moment. 'And I wonder if you felt very alone?'

Squirrel glanced away and bowed his head. There was a moment of quiet and then he gasped.

'Look,' he said, pointing to the ground.

Hare followed his direction and there, in a glimmer of light, was a seedling, its stem grown long and thin and its leaves yellow as it strained towards the light.

'It's been here all this time,' Squirrel said as if to himself, his voice full of wonder.

'It was safe here,' Hare said.

Squirrel gulped. 'And so alone.'

Hare nodded. 'I know,' she replied.

Squirrel's chest heaved as he took a few tentative hops toward it.

'It's so weak, Hare,' he said, his voice beginning to break.

'And strong,' Hare added. 'It did well to survive.'

Taking a breath, Squirrel bent down and gently scooped the seedling up with a handful of soil. He looked at it quietly, his eyes beginning to fill with tears. Standing carefully, he turned to Hare and handed her the tiny, fragile thing.

'Will you help me?' he whispered, as finally his tears began to fall.

Hare held hers back as she took the seedling from him and

replied, 'Of course.'

Squirrel smiled and said, 'Shall we go home?'

The path from the oak tree was straight from there on, and soon they stepped out of the dark wood into the warmth of the sun. Recognising the meadow close to where they had first met, they found a place near a babbling brook where soft light streamed through a nearby wood, and together they planted the seedling.

'I remember burying it now,' Squirrel said. 'It was the coldest and darkest of days.'

'Is it the thing you were searching for?' Hare asked.

Squirrel lay back on the soft grass and closed his eyes. As always, Hare stayed nearby, nibbling on a patch of sweet clover. Soothed by the rhythm of her gentle lollop, Squirrel took a deep breath and then he smiled.

'I have found it, Hare,' he said.

Hare turned to look at him and sat back on her haunches, munching a mouthful of leaves, waiting for him to go on.

'But it wasn't the seedling,' Squirrel continued.

'What was it?' Hare asked.

Squirrel frowned a little. 'I'm not sure,' he said.

Hare nodded her head slowly, as if thinking carefully. 'What's it like?' she said.

Squirrel smiled. 'Just like I thought it would be. Like being warm on the inside,' he replied.

'That's a good feeling,' Hare said, her eyes shining like she could feel it too.

Squirrel stretched out on the grass, soaking up the remains of the sun, while Hare continued to munch and lollop. After a time, Hare stopped and said, 'Do you know where you found it?'

Squirrel yawned as he turned on his side, curled up on the soft, warm earth and considered her question. Hare lay down to rest close by and as she became quiet with her thoughts, Squirrel began to drift into sleep. Opening his heavy eyes, he looked at Hare.

'It was along the way,' he said.

Hare smiled as Squirrel knew she would. Sleepy with the warmth of the sun on the inside, he thought of the day they first met, how he'd squealed with fright, how he'd been scared of her … how he'd been scared of everyone. It all made so much sense now. Squirrel smiled at Hare.

'Somewhere along the way with you,' he said.

A Story About Attachment

Squirrel has difficulties with attachment.

You may not have heard the word 'attachment' before – at least, not used in this way. There are different types of attachment. Attachment describes the way we have learnt to be when we are with other people. We can learn to be one way with certain people and another with different people. Different attachment relationships have different names. We tend to have an attachment style, a sort of default position. Squirrel's attachment style in this story is called 'avoidant'.

When we avoid things, we stay away from them. When life is hard and people are unkind or cruel to us, or when they scold us or make fun of us for showing our feelings, it can make sense to stay away from our emotions and other people. After all, it is hard to tell who might hurt us and who might not. Our attachments can be different with different people, and our default style can change over time. For example, a person might become more like Squirrel if someone starts to bully them.

Squirrel has learnt to stay away from his feelings and keep other animals at a distance because of what happened to him in the long, cold winter. Sometimes, he uses anger to keep animals away. He has learnt to be independent and not ask for help.

What do you think about being independent and not asking for help? Do you think it's always a good thing to just rely on yourself, or do you think it's good to be able to ask for help? When Squirrel meets Hare, he isn't sure whether to stay or go. Why do you think that is?

It can be helpful to think of having different parts of ourselves. Imagine it is the first time you're going ice skating or staying away from home on a school trip. A part of you might be excited and another part might be scared. If you think no one will understand the part of you that feels scared, you might decide to keep it hidden. It can make sense to hide your feelings sometimes. The problem is that when we shut away our feelings all or most of the time, we can start to feel lonely and empty, like a part of us is missing.

Squirrel has hidden the sad, scared and hopeful parts of himself. Other parts have been left to get on with the job of living life. Sometimes, we call these parts the coping part. When Squirrel meets Hare, he has already learnt that it isn't safe to show his feelings. Hare seems different in a good way to him, but he finds it difficult to trust anyone. Because he can't be sure if she is different, he finds it hard to decide whether to stay or go.

Why do you think we feel lonely and empty when we shut away our feelings? What does it feel like to share your feelings with someone kind that you trust?

Squirrel is looking for something that is missing. He describes it as feeling warm, like having the sun on the inside.

It is tricky for Squirrel when he meets Hare. He feels safer when he keeps his feelings inside and other animals at a distance, but when he does that, he feels lonely and empty. He doesn't know whether to trust Hare or not. When people have been unkind or cruel to us, it can be tough to trust anyone to care for our feelings and not hurt us. In the story, Squirrel sees something different about Hare. At first, he feels a bit confused and thinks she is a bit weird, but slowly he starts to trust her and together, they go on a journey. The wood is a metaphor for Squirrel's past, and the old oak tree represents the place where he has hidden the sad, scared and hopeful parts of himself. The seedling represents these parts. When he trusts Hare enough to share this part with her – and she responds with kindness – he begins to heal.

Do you think it helps to talk to someone you trust about what has happened to you? Have you ever shared a painful memory? How did it feel? When Hare asks him where he found 'it', why do you think Squirrel says, 'It was somewhere along the way with you'?

Squirrel learnt to hide his feelings for good reason. It wouldn't have been sensible or safe to show them to Hare until he could be sure that she would be kind and accepting of them. Little by little, as they journey together, he begins to understand that he doesn't need to be scared of Hare, he can trust her. When he trusts her enough, he is able to reveal his past and show her his most vulnerable feelings. In this way, he has discovered who Hare really is – a kind, trustworthy animal, rather than the frightening animal he thought she was at the beginning of the story. He is expressing that with her help, he has found enough trust to make connections. The connection fills him with a feeling of warmth, whereas before he had felt lonely and empty ... like something was missing.

To some extent, we all keep parts of ourselves hidden.

Why do you think we all keep parts of ourselves hidden? Can you think of times when you've chosen not to show your feelings?

It can sometimes be sensible not to show your feelings. Not everyone can be trusted with them, for example, people who laugh at your feelings or tell you that they're silly or don't matter.

Who can't you trust with your feelings? Who can you trust?

Go to page 121 to learn more about attachment and some simple practices that can help.

Four
Beautiful Tail

Even though Rat's heart ached, she smiled kindly as she peeked out from beneath the park bench. For a moment, the sun had broken through the thick, grey cloud. A little girl in a red raincoat was toddling amongst a sea of yellow flowers, giggling and laughing as she watched Squirrel frolicking in the glistening grass. The little girl's mother was kneeling beside her, pointing at Squirrel.

'Isn't he lovely?' the mother said. 'Look at his beautiful tail.'

Rat sighed as she looked down at her own long, hairless tail. It was anything but beautiful. Her chest heaved and she stepped a little further back into the darkness.

'Gotcha!'

A stick with a sharp metal point shot past Rat's head, narrowly missed her throat and grazed her shoulder. Rat squealed with pain and jumped into the light with her teeth bared, ready to fight. The park attendant jabbed at her again as the mother screamed. The little girl froze for a second, her eyes darting in Rat's direction, and then she opened her mouth wide and began to cry.

With a pain in her heart worse than the pain in her shoulder, Rat ran. She ran out of the park and straight into the road. A car screeched to a halt, and a man began to shout as his dog slipped its lead and began to give chase. With the barking dog nipping at her heels, Rat ran. The breath in her throat burned, and her whole body pounded as the blood raced through her veins, and still, she ran. Darting down the first street and up the next, she took a sharp left, bounded up a flight of concrete steps and squeezed nimbly under a metal gate. The barking dog came to a grinding halt as Rat scurried into the garden and hid in the hedge.

This wasn't the first time this had happened to Rat. She lay on the damp earth and caught her breath as the baffled dog stood panting in the driveway, desperately trying to force its huge head through the railings. A crow cawed as it circled in the sky above, and the dog barked up at it, distracted. Rat cowered and retreated further into the hedge as the confused dog cocked its leg on the gate before turning and trotting back down the steps. Rat chuckled quietly and stretched out, feeling the relief of her escape and the warmth of the sun on her back. It was then she felt something pressing on her tail. She spun around to see a paw pinning her to the ground.

'Hello, Rat,' Cat purred in a sly voice. 'Been in the wars, have we?'

Rat froze for a moment, and her heart began to pound again. She struggled, trying to pull her tail free.

'Let me go!' she shouted.

Cat laughed. 'Like this?' she said, lifting her paw and releasing her grip for a second, only to slam it straight back down harder, digging her claws into Rat's flesh.

Rat twisted and turned, using all her strength to try and wriggle free, but it was no use. She turned to glare at Cat, the tears welling in her eyes.

'Going to cry now, are you?' Cat teased. 'Boohoo, poor little Rat.' She raised her voice, pretending to shout out. 'Anyone care about poor little Rat?'

Cat looked around as if waiting for someone to come forward with a reply.

'No, seems not, I'm afraid, Rat,' she sighed with a smile. 'No one cares about a stupid little creature like you.'

Cat brought her face close to Rat's and when she spoke, her voice was low.

'So, let that be a lesson to you, Rat. Lucky for you, I've just had my lunch, but if you ever come into my garden again, I'll eat you for pudding. Do you hear?'

Tears streaming down her face, Rat wanted to fight back but somehow she couldn't. Cat was right. She was stupid. Stupid and useless. She looked away.

'There you go, what a good little rat,' Cat said with disdain, then she snarled, 'Now run, you coward!'

So, Rat ran. She ran out of the garden, back across the road, through the park, out of the town and through the fields all the way down to the river. But she didn't stop there. She crossed the disused wooden bridge with its rotten planks and broken railings strewn with bits of string and rope from years of shoddy repairs. She ran along the riverbank, past a tree that had fallen into the water, its long branches trailing like tentacles in the fast-flowing water. She ran over the pipe draining the water from the farmer's fields and up into the wood beyond.

Only then did Rat stop. She crawled into a hole in amongst a pile of moss-covered logs and fell asleep, exhausted.

Rat awoke to the morning light and the sound of the rain falling through the trees. Careful not to show herself, she peeked out through the logs.

'Rain again, Badger,' Rabbit called as she hopped through the long grass, her six baby bunnies skipping and jumping around her feet.

'Got your hands full there, Rabbit,' Badger chuckled amiably.

Badger looked in Rat's direction as if sensing someone was watching. Rat ducked down, not wanting to be seen. Badger took a couple of steps in her direction. Rat held her breath.

'Morning, Badger,' Fox called.

Badger waved and smiled. 'Another wet one,' he said. 'I'm not sure the river can hold much more.'

Fox looked across the field and down to the water. She lifted her gaze to the sky and sniffed the air.

'Drier days are coming, Badger,' she said. 'I can smell it.'

Then, a puzzled look crossed her face, and she sniffed the air again.

'Hello,' she said. 'Who's that?'

Fox looked at Badger and then across to where Rat was hiding. She took a couple of steps in Rat's direction and so, knowing that Fox would find her, Rat stepped into the light. She looked down at her feet, moving only her eyes to glance up at Badger and Fox. Every inch of her body trembled, but she tried to look like she wasn't bothered at all.

'Hello, Rat,' Fox said, her voice calm and kind. 'What brings you to this part of the world?'

Rat tried to speak but somehow, she couldn't find any words. Heart beating in her throat, she shrugged. She wanted to say something. She tried to speak, but her mind was blank. She glanced up and could see Badger looking at her, waiting expectantly.

Rat took a deep breath but –

'Morning, Fox. Morning, Badger,' Hare called.

They turned to look at her, and Rat's shoulders dropped. Seeing their bright-eyed smiles as the friends greeted each other, she stepped back into the darkness and watched as they walked away.

You should've said something, you should've smiled, the voice in Rat's head grumbled at her. *They must think you're so stupid, so rude.*

Feeling pressure in her chest like she was being crushed by Cat's jaws, Rat flopped to the ground. There was no place for her here, no place for her anywhere.

Why can't you just be normal and say hello? No wonder

nobody likes you.

Her thoughts were interrupted by three short, sharp raps on the wood. Rat's ears pricked up, and she listened.

Rat-a-tat tat. There it was again. Rat got slowly to her feet and crept towards the sound.

'CAW!'

The sound burst into the silence as the crow's head burst in between the logs. Rat jumped and squealed.

'Hello, Rat,' Crow said. 'Saw you get in last night ... of caw- of course!'

He looked at Rat with his bright black eyes for a moment, then he pulled his head back out of the hole with a flurry of feathers before poking it back through and throwing something in Rat's direction.

'Thought you might be glad of that, you just having moved in and all that, of course.'

Rat glanced down to see a large piece of tasty-looking bread.

'Got it from the old woman at number forty-four. Not that she puts it out for me, of caw-course! That'd be for Robin and his smart red breast ... of caw- of course. Still, all the same. Staying long? I should introduce you to Mouse. Friendly folks round here, of course!'

Crow chatted on, and Rat listened, full of wonder. How easily Crow talked. It was almost as if he didn't mind Rat being quiet. As if Crow didn't mind her just being there. Rat felt lighter somehow, like she could breathe again.

'You don't mind?' Rat asked suddenly.

Crow stopped and tilted his head. 'What's that, Rat?' he said curiously.

'That the old woman at number forty-four doesn't put the bread out for you?'

'Hmm ...' Crow thought for a moment. 'Strange sorts, humans. Seems to me they like everything ... hmmm ...,' he paused and turned his head from side to side, 'the way they think it should be. Not much room for anything else then, of caw-course.'

Crow smiled. 'You seem like a nice sort, Rat. You should fit in well here. Enjoy the bread ... of course.'

Then, with another flurry of feathers, Crow was gone.

Rat's heart had leapt when she heard Crow's kind words, but now he was gone and Rat was left with nothing but the empty space. It didn't take long for the voice in her head to start whispering again:

He doesn't mean it. He wouldn't have said it ... not if he knew you.

So, the days came and they went. The rain stayed, and Rat kept to the shadows. Occasionally, she saw one of the woodland animals and although she preferred to remain hidden, when she heard them talking and laughing, her heart ached.

Then one morning, when Rat was sitting quietly, she heard a scream. Rat peered out of her hole to see the animals gathered at the edge of the wood, looking towards the river as if frozen with terror. Rat ran to join them and followed their line of sight. Rabbit was on the riverbank, hopping frantically and wailing. One of her babies, Little Rabbit, had fallen into the water.

Rat looked from Fox to Hare to Badger and then back to the river. Hare and Fox started to run towards Rabbit and Little Rabbit, but Rat knew it was no use. The river was flowing too fast. Rat turned around and ran in the opposite direction.

Fox and Hare arrived at the riverbank together, but as fast as they'd been, it was too late. Little Rabbit had been swept further down the widening river by the raging water and was out of reach. Without a thought, Fox jumped into the water but was immediately sucked down, tossed and turned by the eddying currents. Hare splashed in after her. Holding onto the branch of a tree, she managed to haul Fox out. They turned and looked despairingly after the tiny rabbit, just as Rat emerged out of the land drain further along the bank.

Keeping an eye on the little rabbit in the river, Rat ran as if she had a dog on her tail and leapt onto the fallen tree. Then, using her powerful tail to help her balance, she nimbly made her way along the trailing branches that danced amongst the

rapids, way out into the middle of the water just as Little Rabbit came hurtling towards her. Rat knew she had to time her jump just right. Otherwise, Little Rabbit would sweep right past her. She readied herself, then hesitated for a moment – a moment longer than she should have – then, she leapt into the river.

The water surged around her and Rat flailed as she tried to grab hold of Little Rabbit, but her fur was as soft and smooth as silk. Rat grabbed at her ear, but it slipped through her fingers. Little Rabbit had gone.

Just then, she felt a tug on her tail from down in the depths.

She dived under the water and grasped hold of Little Rabbit, pulling her to the surface. The little one gasped for air as they were swept onwards down the river. Rat looked behind her. She was a powerful swimmer, but she knew she couldn't beat the current. She'd known it all along. But she also knew the dilapidated bridge with its broken ropes was up ahead. Rat held Little Rabbit under her chin to keep her face above the water, and just before the current swept them under the bridge, Rat launched herself into the air using every bit of her might and grabbed hold of one of the dangling ropes with her teeth.

Using both paws, she pulled Little Rabbit out of the water and pushed her up onto the bridge, where she fell coughing and spluttering.

With Little Rabbit safe, Rat pulled herself up and flopped onto the wooden planks beside her, just as Hare, Fox and Rabbit arrived.

Rat looked up to see their faces full of horror at wet Little Rabbit coughing and she knew, just knew, this was all her fault. *If she'd run faster, or thought quicker, or hadn't hesitated, this would never have happened. She is such a stupid, stupid rat!* And with that thought, Rat jumped up and ran. She ran and ran until, at last, she fell into a hole beneath a stone and sobbed.

It was Crow that found her, with a familiar *rat-a-tat tat.*

'Hello, Rat,' he said. 'Been quite a day, hasn't it? Never seen anything quite like that … of course.'

Rat looked up but didn't say anything.

'I could hardly believe my eyes, of course, when you jumped out of that drain. I said to Pigeon, "She must have known, Pigeon! She must have worked it out." Crow chuckled. 'And to think we say "as the crow flies". Perhaps we should say "as the rat runs!" He cocked his head and looked at Rat with his curious eye. 'So did you, Rat?'

Rat sniffed, wiped her eyes, pulled herself out of her hole and sat on the grass. 'What?' she said.

'Work it out, of course?'

Rat thought. 'Well, I could see the river was flowing fast.'

'Of course, of caw-course. And by the time Fox and Hare got there, poor Little Rabbit would have been swept into a wider part of the river?'

Rat nodded. 'Yes, and they wouldn't be able to reach her.'

'And the drain?' Crow said, tilting his head in the opposite direction.

'I knew it was a shortcut, and it would bring me out close to the old tree that had fallen into the water.'

'Of course ... and the bridge?'

'I'd seen the rope dangling in the water. I thought I could grab it with my teeth.'

'Of course, of caw-course. I knew it, just knew it,' Crow said. 'What an intelligent sort you are, Rat. And fast and strong. Those teeth, those jaws. I said that to Pigeon too.'

'And brave. Don't forget brave, Crow,' a voice said.

Rat and Crow looked around to see Fox with Hare at her side.

Fox smiled at them.

'Of course, of course,' Crow said. 'Rat, the hero. "That leap!" I said to Pigeon. "That leap, Pigeon!"'

'Why did you run?' Fox said.

Rat hung her head. 'I hesitated,' she said.

'Before you leapt?' Crow asked.

Rat nodded. 'Little Rabbit nearly drowned, and it's all my fault.'

'Nearly drowned, of course,' Crow said. 'But not *your* fault … of course.'

Rat looked up.

'Not your fault at all, never been your fault … of course.'

'What do you mean?' Rat said.

'I said to Pigeon, "The things I've seen!" I'm up above the town, looking down, of course. I saw it all. Stop blaming yourself. None of it was your fault … of caw-course. Nothing wrong with you. A decent sort.'

'A very decent sort,' Fox echoed. 'You saved her, Rat. You saved Little Rabbit.'

Rat looked at their earnest faces, still doubting them. It was then that Rabbit arrived.

'What I didn't see of your marvellous rescue, Little Rabbit told us,' Rabbit said, nodding down at her little one. 'Thank you, Rat. You saved her.'

The little one blinked, and Rat blinked back. Little Rabbit leapt into Rat's arms, laughing and giggling, then wrapped her arms around Rat's neck and squeezed her like she would never let go. Rat hugged her back, and Little Rabbit clambered down Rat's tummy and grabbed hold of her tail.

'Look, Mummy,' she said, beaming with delight. 'It saved me. Rat's tail. Isn't it beautiful?'

As Hare and Fox watched, Rabbit came to stand beside her little one.

'It is, sweetheart,' she said. 'It's the most beautiful tail in the whole world.'

And Rat began to cry again, but it was a different sort of tears this time. They were tears of relief and joy. *Perhaps Crow is right. There is nothing wrong with her. Absolutely nothing at all.*

A Story About Shame

Rat experiences shame.

What is shame? How would you explain it to someone?

Shame is a normal feeling (it might cause a sick feeling in our stomach and a tight or heavy feeling in our chest). Some people believe that in small amounts, shame can help us to fit in with others. For example, if you say something mean to a friend and hurt them, you might feel some shame which might stop you from doing it again. The problem is we can also feel shame when we haven't done anything wrong.

Do you think Rat has done anything wrong? Why do you think the mother screams in the park and the little girl cries when they see Rat?

When people mistreat us because of the way we look, feel, think or what we believe, we can feel shame. They might give us the message that we shouldn't feel the way we do, think what we do, do what we do or be who we are! They might laugh at us, be cruel or express disgust. Rat hasn't done anything wrong, but she still feels shame.

Why do you think Rat felt shame? What has happened to her?

Shame makes us feel like something is wrong with us. It is like we are unlovable, not enough as we are or don't belong. Rat has been treated very badly in the town she lives in. The humans react with horror and disgust when they see her. Other animals, such as Cat and the dog, try to chase, bully and hurt her. Rat feels shame because of the way she has been treated. She thinks there is something wrong with her.

Do you think it's right that Rat feels this way?

There is nothing wrong with Rat. In fact, she has many strengths. She is clever, fast and strong. She only feels shame because of the way she has been treated. To escape feeling shame, we might hide or try very hard to please other people and not make any mistakes. This can be exhausting!

What does Rat do to try and protect herself from further feelings of shame?

Rat tries to hide to avoid further feelings of shame. If no one can see her, no one can hurt her. Think about what happens when Rat escapes from the town.

What changes when Rat reaches the wood? How do the other animals treat her? Can you think of any real 'human' world examples of something that could happen that are similar?

Rat continues to keep out of the way even though the other animals in the wood seem to accept her.

Why do you think Rat continues to keep out of the way, even when the other animals seem to accept her?

Rat is used to humans and other animals mistreating her. It is understandable that she finds it difficult to trust the animals in the wood.

Bullying can cause shame. Shame also makes us bully ourselves. We might think unkind thoughts about ourselves, or believe others are thinking them, such as 'I'm stupid', 'Everyone hates me', 'I'm worthless', or 'I'm no good'.

Do you ever say mean things about yourself either out loud or in your head? How does it make you feel? Would you say those things to a friend? Why not? How did Rat bully herself?

If we bully ourselves, we can find it hard to believe when we find others who are kind and accept us for who we are. Like Rat, we might think that people don't really mean the kind things they say, or we might think they are only pretending to like and accept us. It can feel safer to think that way as we don't want to risk getting hurt again. That means shame can take a long time to heal. Rat tells herself she is stupid and useless. She thinks the other animals will see her as rude and strange.

In truth, Rat is brave, strong, fast and clever. Because of these strengths, she rescues Little Rabbit when the other animals couldn't. But even then, she still believes the other animals will blame her and hate her. It's not surprising – that was how she was treated when she was in the town.

What feelings do you think Rat has at the end of the story? Has she changed at all, or is it just the way she feels about herself?

If we have too much shame, we have to find others who are kind to us and a way to be kind to ourselves. We have to find a way to stop telling ourselves we are not good enough. Like Rat at the end of the story, it is important to be proud of who you are.

Do you ever feel too much shame? Have you got any ideas about how you might help yourself or someone else who feels shame? What are you proud of? What are your strengths?

Go to page 127 to learn more about shame and some simple practices that can help.

FIVE
Whispers

Owl's short but clear hoot echoed through the wood just as the sun was rising. Fox froze and listened to Owl's message. Pain gripped her like a razor-sharp claw digging into her heart. Her mind went blank, and time seemed to slow down. The mist drifted lazily over the frosty grass, and Crow soared silently in the shimmering sky. The birds continued their chatter and a cold, fresh breeze rippled through Fox's fur as she stood, motionless, feeling like she was trying to recall something she had never known. Owl called again, more urgently. Fox's heart gave an enormous thump, and she began to run.

She ran as only Fox could run. Going around and around in her head were the words, *It's too soon. I'm too far away.* With each repetition, she pushed herself just a little further, to go just a little faster. She could make it. If she ran fast enough, she could still make it.

Soon Fox could see the wood. All that stood in her way was one more hedge and one more field. She'd jump. She'd done it before, she'd do it again. She leapt, clearing the top with inches to spare and then gasped in surprise – there was Baby Rabbit caught in a trap.

His terrified squeal shot through Fox, seeming to scrape at her bones. She fell, breathing fast, her heart pounding. She righted herself, ready to run. Then, as she glanced at Baby Rabbit, to the wood and back to Baby Rabbit again, Fox let out an agonising howl.

Baby Rabbit screeched with fright, and Fox took a deep breath, steadying herself.

'It's okay. It's going to be okay,' she said, gently going to his aid.

'I'm sorry, Fox,' Baby Rabbit said as he coughed and cried.

'It's not your fault,' Fox said, her heart beating fast.

Baby Rabbit was caught up in something. Something stupid the humans had created. Fox had seen it before in the rivers and in the woods. She thought frantically, trying to work out the best way of releasing Baby Rabbit from the plastic noose that had looped around his neck.

She pulled at the plastic with her teeth, and Baby Rabbit squealed in pain. She stopped. Her chest tightening, Fox tried to stop her rising panic and think. Baby Rabbit would be fine. He was well and truly stuck but not in any danger. Not from the plastic at least, she thought as she looked to the skies. She should go, come back later. Get Pigeon to take a message to Mother Rabbit. She turned and started to run and then she

looked back … right into Baby Rabbit's sad, dejected eyes. Fox growled as she came to a halt, every fibre of her body tensed. She couldn't do it, she couldn't just leave him there. She took a deep breath and retraced her steps.

Ears drooping, Baby Rabbit looked at her and did his best to smile. Fox did her best to smile back and took a moment to assess the situation. One end of the plastic was caught in the spiky hedge and the other around Baby Rabbit's neck. There was only one thing for it.

She bit and pawed at the hedge, the thorns of the brambles sticking in her paws and mouth. Finally, the branch broke, the plastic unfurled and as it loosened around his neck, Baby Rabbit wriggled free, threw his arms around Fox and hugged her tight.

'Go home, Baby Rabbit,' she said. 'I have to run.'

And run she did.

Fox ran faster than she'd ever done before, across the fallow field and up the hill and even though her paws hurt and her heart was pounding, she never slowed. Not even as she ran through the wood, bounding over the trunks of fallen trees, did she slow. The words, *I'm coming, hang on, please hang on*, pushed her on and on.

When she reached the edge of the clearing, she stopped. Hare was walking towards her with her ears hanging low.

Fox shook her head. 'No.'

Hare came closer, and Fox could see the tears in her eyes.

'No. I ran all the way,' Fox said.

Hare reached out her paw. 'Fox ...' she said kindly.

Fox pulled away, glancing at the small group of animals gathered in a circle a short distance ahead. Eyes wide open, she looked back to Hare and shook her head again. Then, as Hare called after her, she turned and ran back the way she had come.

Fox ran without thinking, not knowing where she was going or why but feeling like she might burst if she stopped. Before long, her legs began to burn, and still she pushed on until she realised she was heading towards the moor. Little by little, the fields were growing larger and the hedgerows fewer and further between. Fox ran on and on. As the mist continued to roll in, thickening to fog, it gently enveloped her, amplifying her every breath and beat of her heart. Then, she saw it – the old wall. The small hole within the pile of dislodged stones. There, right before her.

Slowing to a walk, Fox's heart lurched into her throat, she

drew closer to it. Her heart beating louder and faster with each step. The gap was smaller than she remembered. The scent caught in her nostrils as she stepped inside, taking her back there like it was happening now. She glanced outside, longing to see that graceful shadow, to hear those words. *Stay down.*

Feeling like her heart had grown so large in her chest it might break her apart, Fox lay down on the warm, dry earth, curled herself up into a ball and fell asleep.

She awoke to a sharp *rat-a-tat-tat* and looked out to see Crow.

'What are you doing here?' she said, a pain gnawing at her insides.

Crow peered at her with a beady eye. 'Looking for you, of course,' he said.

Feeling irritated but not fully understanding why, Fox held her breath and closed her eyes for a moment.

'And why, exactly, are you looking for me?' she asked, forcing the words between her teeth.

Crow ruffled his feathers and blinked. 'Because we'd lost you, of course,' he said. 'And you? What are you doing here?'

Fox could feel the pressure building up inside her like she might explode. Staring at the ground, her lip started to curl as she did her best to hold back a snarl.

Crow blinked again. 'You've lost someone too, of course,' he said.

Fox glared at him then and the words shot from her mouth. 'The difference is he's not here, is he, Crow?'

Crow flinched as the words hit him. 'Of course, of course. This is the wrong place.'

Fox continued her attack.

'The problem is, Crow, there's no right place. Stag's not here, he's not anywhere and he never will be,' she shouted, her voice beginning to break.

Crow paused and spoke kindly. 'He was once, of course. He was here for you. Always was.'

Fox gulped as the anger shifted within her, changing, pushing up through her body as if trying to force tears from her eyes. As she tried to speak, the words seemed to stick in her throat and her voice became no more than a whisper.

'That's the thing, Crow. I wasn't there for Stag. When he needed me, I wasn't there. I shouldn't have stopped to help Baby Rabbit.'

Crow thought for a second, then said, 'Not much choice, of

course.'

Fox took a breath. 'No, Crow. It's my fault and now I can never, ever put it right,' she said.

Silence fell between them, and Fox strained to hear the whispers of the wind in the grass. At last, she looked up at Crow and sighed.

'I'm sorry, I shouldn't have snapped at you. None of this is your fault,' she said.

Crow tilted his head from side to side. 'No need to be sorry … of course.'

Fox smiled sadly. 'I am, all the same.'

Crow took a moment to look around. 'This is where you met?'

'More like where we didn't meet,' Fox replied. 'I do wish I could have seen him that day, Crow. He told me that the hounds were already tired from chasing me and it was easy to get ahead of them, jump a river and throw them off the scent.'

Fox paused and chuckled softly. 'Can you imagine, Crow? Easy? He said it was easy.'

Crow laughed and tilted his head as he thought. 'Easier to imagine than those creatures with long necks and black and white stripes, of course. The creatures he said Osprey told him about, who lived in a hot land far away.'

Fox furrowed her brow. 'A creature with a long neck ... *and* stripes?' she asked.

'I'm not sure,' Crow said, and Fox laughed as she tried to imagine what it would look like. Shaking her head and looking back up at where Stag's shadow had arched overhead, Fox sighed.

'He had so many stories, didn't he, Crow?'

'Of course,' Crow said. 'I think I heard them all.' He looked sideways at Fox. 'At least twice, of course.'

Fox laughed and then paused. Stag had lived such a long and interesting life.

'Will you tell the others you found me and I'm okay?' she said.

'Of course. And Hare has something to tell you, of course,' Crow replied.

Fox looked up. 'What is it?'

Crow flapped his wings. 'Not for me to say, of course,' he said.

Then, glancing around at the moor, he spread his enormous wings, took a hop and a step before soaring into the sky and calling down, 'There is a right place, of course.'

Fox watched him go, skipping and dancing in the wind,

drifting further and further away until he disappeared from sight. For a moment, she stared after him at the space he had left behind. She wasn't sure what he meant, but she was sure this wasn't the right place. There was no point in staying. For a moment, she looked back at the emptiness of the old stone wall and then with a heavy heart, stepped into the dense fog and began the long walk home.

Fox couldn't see the sun, but she knew it must be late as the light was getting low and the bitter cold was piercing her fur. Even though she had been walking for hours, she kept going, putting one paw in front of another. Finding her way in the dense fog was proving impossible and the more she walked, the more tired she became. She didn't seem to be getting anywhere, and she was starting to think she was walking in circles, going around and around.

Suddenly, like she'd hit an invisible wall, she stopped. She couldn't do it. She couldn't keep going any longer. She searched the fog-laden landscape and realised that she was lost ... and completely and utterly alone.

It was then it came. At first, like the slow beat of a velvet drum. Fox's ears twitched as she strained her eyes to peer through the rolling waves of the misty sea. The loudening beat of the drum was joined by a steady *huff, huff, huff.* Fox held her breath. And then, as if out of nowhere, he appeared, slipping from the shadow into the light.

Fox gasped. Their eyes met as Stag's warm breath bellowed into the cold air.

Fox blinked, standing perfectly still, hardly daring to breathe for fear the moment wouldn't last, that she would lose him again. There had been so much she'd wanted to say, things she should have said before he died. She'd wanted to tell him how grateful she was for everything he'd done, for saving her and how, more than anything in the world, she'd wanted to be there at the end. But at that moment, she understood it came down to just one thing.

Fox whispered, 'I love you.'

Stag held her gaze for a moment. The moor fell silent and the grass seemed to whisper back, *I love you too.* Then, with a nod of his head and a stamp of his hoof, Stag was gone. Gone in the single beat of a bumblebee's wing.

Fox's chest heaved as she gasped for breath. She looked around, but there was nothing to be seen, nothing to be heard.

She called out Stag's name, her voice echoing across the moor. In the silence that answered, she began to feel scared. The fog was closing in around her. Stag was gone, and she was lost and alone. As her heart began to thump, Fox heard Crow call down to her.

'Follow me home.'

Fox looked up to see him hovering close by, feathers fluttering in the wind. Needing no further persuasion, she started to run. With Crow as her compass, Fox sped across the moor, through the fields, back to the wood and into the clearing where Hare was waiting for her. Fox ran to her and as Hare embraced her tightly, she began to cry.

As Fox's sobs became quieter, Hare pulled away from her a little, gently lifting her face to look at her.

'He spoke to me, Fox, just before he died,' she said. 'I wanted to tell you before you turned and ran.'

Fox looked at her, stifling another sob as it began to rise. 'What did he say?' she said.

'With his final breath, he whispered, "Tell Fox she never left my side."'

Fox gulped. 'What did he mean, Hare?'

'Close your eyes, Fox,' Hare said.

Fox closed her eyes.

'Now, look into your heart and tell me what you find there.'

For a moment, Fox searched, then with a gasp, she opened her eyes.

'Stag,' she said.

Hare smiled. 'You were with him in his heart, Fox, right to the end. And he will always be with you, in yours.'

Hare pulled Fox close again and held her as her tears continued to fall. Fox closed her eyes and looked back inside. Now she understood what Crow had meant. She had been looking in the wrong place. Stag wasn't on the moor. He was here in her heart and so was the love he had left behind. The understanding seemed to push a fresh torrent of tears from her eyes but slowly, inevitably, they began to subside and as they did, Hare loosened her hold.

Crow and Owl glided silently down to rest beside them and, one by one, the other animals joined. Badger, Mouse, Squirrel, Rat, Mother Rabbit, Little Rabbit, Baby Rabbit, Pigeon – they were all there. Staying close, they walked together to the place where Stag's giant, gentle body lay. They stood, each of them

with their memories, many of happy days and some of sad.

Hare was the first to step forward. Tenderly, she gathered a pile of the golden leaves from the forest floor and scattered them over Stag's body so they gently enveloped him. Badger was next, and one by one they took their turn, until it came to Fox.

All that remained uncovered was Stag's noble head, his eyes closed as if in a peaceful sleep. Using her snout, she carefully nuzzled the leaves over him. As the last of him disappeared from sight, she whispered, 'I love you' and the wind blew. A shadow appeared to arch gracefully overhead and as one, the animals looked to the sky and began to cheer and bellow and cry, their hearts filled not only with sadness but with the greatest of joy.

A STORY ABOUT LOSS AND GRIEF

Fox is experiencing grief following the death of Stag.

Grief is something we feel when a loved one dies, or we lose someone or something we care about. It is normal and natural. That doesn't mean it's easy. The pain of loss usually gets less over time, although most people will have good days and bad days.

We can experience many kinds of loss. It might be the death of a person or an animal. It can also be things like a friend moving away or leaving a house or town where we've lived. It could even be losing a favourite toy. In this story, Stag has died and Fox is grieving.

Have you ever lost something or someone you love very much? How did it make you feel?

We feel many things when we grieve and there is no right or wrong way to do it, nor is there a set amount of time it should take. When we experience a significant loss, it is usual to grieve for many years. We might feel lots of emotions and have physical reactions, like not feeling hungry or being unable to sleep.

We often think that grieving means feeling sad, but that's not the only feeling we get when grieving. It is common to feel anger, fear, shock, confusion and guilt. Feeling nothing at all or numb is also common. It is also completely normal to have times when we feel okay and even happy.

What feelings did Fox feel when she heard Stag had died?

One of the things Fox feels is guilt that she didn't get to Stag before he died. She regrets stopping to help Baby Rabbit. Fox also feels some anger and is cross with Crow.

Can you think of other reasons someone might feel guilty if someone dies? What do you think about Fox feeling angry? Do you think she is actually angry with Crow or with someone else?

People frequently hold on to things that remind them of people who have died and often return to places where they felt close to them. It is also normal to dream about them and perhaps have a sense of them being nearby. These things help us to continue to feel connected to the person we love and can help us with grief.

Why do you think Fox went back to the old stone wall where she first met Stag?

It is common after someone dies for those left behind to search for them. We can do this almost without realising it – maybe by looking for a face in a crowd or seeing someone that looks similar and thinking for a moment that it might be the person that died. Crow thinks Fox is looking in the wrong place for Stag.

Do you think Fox is looking in the wrong place? Where does Crow think she should look? What do you think happened on the moor afterwards when Fox sees Stag? Do you think she was dreaming or seeing things, or was it Stag's spirit? What do you think happens after we die?

Whatever our beliefs, it is important to remember that when someone dies, they cannot come back. That doesn't mean we can't continue to feel a connection with them.

Where does Fox find Stag at the end of the story? What do you think Stag meant when he told Hare to tell Fox she never left his side? When a person or an animal dies, what do you think they leave behind?

The author Jeanette Winterson wrote: 'This hole in my heart is in the shape of you. No one else can fit it. Why would I want them to?'

She is saying that when someone we love dies, we don't want to forget them or replace them. It wouldn't feel right. Eventually, we adjust to the loss, but remember, there's no set time for how long this takes. It might only be a matter of months, but it may be many years. However, over time our life grows around the hole in our heart and slowly, the pain lessens.

Go to page 131 to learn more about loss and some simple practices that can help.

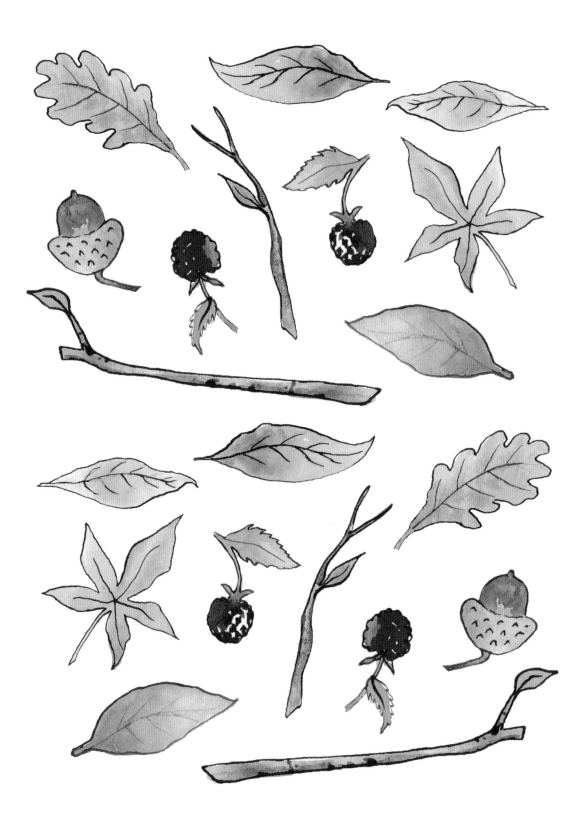

PART II
Behind the Story

ONE
Understanding More About Trauma

THE COURAGEOUS HEART

Trauma can affect anyone of any age. We cannot judge what events might or might not be traumatic based on our own beliefs. It is uniquely personal. As such, the list of potentially traumatic experiences is endless. Overwhelming experiences in which there is often a sense of 'I'm going to die', accompanied by feelings of helplessness, are referred to as 'Big T' traumas by some therapists. When our survival brain perceives we can take action, such as fighting back or running away, we are less likely to experience trauma. When it perceives that we are helpless, and running or fighting is pointless, we shut down. This assessment happens in a moment. The smaller and weaker we are, the more likely it is that our survival brains will perceive that we are helpless. This means the younger we are, the less likely we are to fight or run and the more likely we are to shut down.

Shut down is a state of immobilisation and is common in trauma. We can't move and the mind may cut off from what is happening in the body. When we have repeated experiences of not being able to fight or run, shut down can become a default response to any stressful event. People who experience trauma often blame themselves for not 'doing something' at the time. The truth is this powerful response of the survival brain means they couldn't.

This survival response to a traumatic event has a unique effect on the brain. Some of its functions are compromised, including thinking and memory. If you're about to be eaten by a sabre-toothed tiger, it's probably best not to stop and think about your best course of action! The brain is wired so that the thinking part is bypassed in survival situations. In these moments, we are programmed to react first and ask questions later.

If you've ever been very frightened, you may have noticed how hard, if not impossible, it is to think clearly or speak. Someone recently told me a story of how they were trying to call an ambulance and couldn't remember their address – that's the survival brain!

The brain is a complex organ and our understanding of it is still evolving. It seems that the hippocampus is a part of the brain involved in memory. It organises information, connecting images, thoughts, feelings and sensations to give a clear sense of our experiences. The hippocampus then stores this information as a date-stamped memory, so not only did it happen in the past, but it feels like it happened in the past. In other words, this happened to me, this is when it happened and this is what it was like. We call this an autobiographical memory that is explicit or conscious.

When we are in our survival brain, the hippocampus doesn't function as well. Information stays disconnected and is stored as an implicit or unconscious memory that has no date stamp. Implicit memory is involved in things like being able to ride a bike or play the piano. In this case, it refers to a stimulus that gets a response without any conscious connection to past events.

In trauma, any sights, sounds, smells, tastes or even thoughts, emotions and sensations reminiscent of the traumatic event can act as a stimulus to trigger an implicit memory, resulting in a fight, flight or shut down response. The survival brain's assessment is that if it was dangerous before, it's better to be safe than sorry now. This means a survival response can look irrational or as if it has come from nowhere. We might typically think of a war veteran who automatically jumps for cover on hearing a loud noise.

When suffering trauma, the brain is constantly on the lookout for threat and is primed to react. At the same time, the social thinking brain becomes sleepy. This means we are out of tune with others, our concentration is poor and our cognitive skills are affected, which, in turn, can strain relationships, work and learning.

For anyone living with trauma, directly or indirectly, it is essential to remember that these struggles and behaviours are the result of their brain behaving entirely as expected and don't, in any way, represent a failure or a deficit in personality.

Fox has experienced a 'Big T' trauma. She believed she was going to die, and she felt helpless. Despite her courage and strength, Fox couldn't run further. In the final moment, she shut down and her mind cut itself off from her body. Her hippocampus was unable to integrate the experience, leaving her with no autobiographical memory. All she had were fragmented or disconnected implicit memories of the moment – sights, sounds, smells, sensations, thoughts and feelings. The setting sun and the wispy, yellow grass of the fallow field are reminiscent of such implicit memories. They act as triggers, putting her into a fight-or-flight response, making her anxious and snappy, but she doesn't understand why. The dog barking and the horn blaring act as further triggers, sending her into a full-blown survival panic. This is confusing and distressing for Fox. Her brain has become wired so that she is constantly on the lookout for threat and primed to react. This means she is always on edge, anxious and quick to anger, which strains her relationship with Owl.

At least Owl can see there is more to Fox's anxiety and anger than there initially seems, although she doesn't know exactly what it is. She can point out that there appears to be some sort of pattern and it is her input and kindness that encourages Fox to seek answers.

It is only when Fox meets Stag that she finally remembers everything. She can make sense of what is happening to her and why she does the things she does. Fox starts to see that she is safe now. As Fox's brain starts to make connections, she begins to integrate her experience and put her past in the past, exactly where it belongs.

Changing the Story: What Helps

It is possible to heal from trauma and here are some simple suggestions about the sort of things that might help the road to recovery. If they don't, it's not a sign of failure. Quite often, professional help and support are needed first. It is vital to seek help from a professional when mental health difficulties are having a significant impact on life and affecting daily functioning. The guidance given here is not exhaustive and you will find plenty of information online to supplement it, as well as many valuable organisations that offer specialist help.

Remember that struggling to manage feelings and behaviours is a normal response to trauma. It is the brain behaving as expected. It is not because you or a child is 'bad.' The list below provides an overview of a few soothing strategies that are particularly useful in healing from trauma but can also be used to manage stress levels and reduce feelings of anxiety, fear and anger.

Spend time doing calming activities. When time is tight, little and often can work well. Even taking a moment to focus on your breathing or taking a few deep breaths can help. Find what works. There are no right or wrong answers. Some people find it helpful to spend time outside in nature or go for a walk. Others like to take a warm bath, meditate or use a calming exercise, such as yoga. Alternatively, it might be enjoying the company of a trusted friend or a pet or curling up on the sofa with a blanket and a hot water bottle. Creative activities, such as painting, drawing, writing, cooking or crafting can be useful for some.

Mindfulness practices. These are also worth mentioning as they help reduce stress and anxiety, but again, it doesn't work for everyone.

Listen to music or audio stories. Music is linked to the release of dopamine in the brain. Dopamine helps us feel good, relax and can improve concentration.

Have fun. Do things that have a feel-good factor for you. Sometimes, when we have been struggling with life, we forget the things we used to enjoy. Have you forgotten the things you used to find fun? Can you think back and recall happy times? What did you enjoy – going for a swim, reading a book, baking a cake, going for a walk or to the beach, meeting a friend, drawing, crafting? The list is endless.

Talk. Share your feelings and experiences with someone you trust who is open and accepting.

Use visualisation practices. For example, imagine a happy place in great detail. What can you see, hear, taste, smell and feel? People often think of times on holiday, perhaps lying on a beach or playing in a pool, but it can be anything. It might even be a made-up place. Kids can make up some wonderful worlds. I remember one with chocolate rivers, caramel waterfalls and doughnut rain!

Stick to routines. Doing the same activities, such as getting up or brushing your teeth, at the same time each day gives a sense of safety and control.

Take regular exercise. Exercise is linked with the release of endorphins which are feel-good chemicals that can also help reduce painful feelings.

Focus on your breath. Often when we're tense or frightened, we stop breathing. Bringing attention to your breathing in some way can be helpful. There are lots of techniques. Try different ones to see which ones work best. An easy one is to breathe in for a count of four, hold for a count of seven and breathe out for eight.

Use grounding techniques. Grounding means bringing your attention to the present moment in some way. You could try picking up an object and describing it in as much detail as you can. Is it heavy or light, is it cold or warm, smooth or coarse, what colour is it, what shape? Challenge yourself to recall the words of a song or a poem. Count backwards from 100 or take a short walk and count your steps, listening to the sound they make and noticing how your feet feel as you move. Try finding and naming five items of the same colour. Listen carefully and identify as many sounds as possible, can you hear traffic, birds, people talking, what else? These are just a few ideas and many more techniques can be found online.

Write in a diary. Journaling can have many benefits. By writing down our experiences, we can start to see patterns in our feelings and behaviours and begin to understand ourselves better. We might start to become aware of things that act as triggers for us. The process of writing stuff down can also help by simply 'getting it out'. Some people find it helpful to make a point of keeping a note of things that have happened in their day that brought them happiness or they are grateful for. It might be something really small, such as a robin on the windowsill or the smile someone gave you in the park.

Use positive self-talk. For example, 'I'm safe now, I survived, I am brave and strong. I can do things well.'

Practise progressive muscle relaxation. Starting at your feet and working up your body one muscle group at a time (i.e. lower legs, upper legs, etc.), contract or tense your muscles as you breathe in, hold for five to ten seconds, then release them as you breathe out and relax for ten to twenty seconds. This will relieve tension in the body and help you feel relaxed.

Two
Understanding More About Anxiety and OCD

THE SHADOW MONSTER

Mouse's story is about anxiety and OCD.

Anxiety is another name for worry. A certain amount of worry in life is normal. For example, many of us would feel anxious about an upcoming exam or a presentation. In small amounts, worry and anxiety can be helpful. For instance, it might help us work a little harder or be a little more careful. Anxiety becomes a problem when we find ourselves worrying a lot of the time or when our worries are out of proportion, such as experiencing high anxiety before meeting a good and trusted friend.

Anxiety is a form of fear and part of a fight-or-flight survival response. When we feel anxious, we look for ways to help ourselves feel safe again. We might avoid things, seek reassurance or try and take some sort of control. Thoughts often play a big part in anxiety. Commonly, we can catastrophise, for example, imagining a headache is a brain tumour. Or we might overgeneralise, thinking something such as *I failed one test, so I will fail them all*. 'The Shadow Monster' can be used to talk about several aspects of anxiety, including the role of thoughts and control. It explores in greater depth a particular type of anxiety, known as OCD, or obsessive-compulsive disorder.

Most people have some knowledge of OCD, and I hear clients say things such as 'I'm a bit OCD.' They often refer to a need to have order in their lives, a place for everything and everything in its place, or a tendency to worry about germs, perhaps resulting in a thorough approach to cleaning or personal hygiene. Depending on what is driving these behaviours and the extent to which they impact their life, they may be right. However, OCD isn't something to be taken lightly and it is often poorly understood.

OCD is a condition that can affect adults and children. As the name suggests, it consists of a combination of obsessions and compulsions. The obsessions are intrusive cognitions (thoughts, images, urges, worries or doubts). An intrusive thought might be something along these lines: *Have I knocked someone down in my car* or *brought germs into my house on my shoes that will kill my family?* Images could be of picking up a knife and stabbing someone or of a loved one being killed. Urges might be jumping off a cliff or in front of a train. Doubt could be: *Have I locked the door,* or *have I turned the oven off?* In children, these intrusive thoughts often relate to the death of parents. Other common obsessions include harming others, worries about being sick, doing something wrong or telling lies.

With OCD, these cognitions repeatedly pop into the mind and due to their nature, can cause extreme anxiety and distress.

As you can probably see, some of these thoughts or worries are more irrational or 'out there' than the more real-life worries experienced in general anxiety. Thoughts such as *Have I locked the door* or *turned the oven off?* might seem more every day, but in OCD, there will be a connection to a disastrous outcome, for example: *Have I locked the door? If not, someone might come into my house and kill my family.*

Everyone gets thoughts of this kind, but for most people, even though they might be unpleasant or cause some mild discomfort, they don't cause any significant anxiety or distress and they don't cause compulsions. What is the difference between someone who is distressed by a thought and someone who isn't?

The answer is in the importance given to the thought and the meaning attached to it. The thought *Have I locked the door?* is one that we may all have had at one time or another. It is sensible to secure your home. Believing your family will die if you haven't is a different matter. There is an overestimation of risk. The meaning given to this thought might be something such as *I've imagined my family dead. Maybe I want them to die. Having this thought must make me a bad person.* These thoughts drive an emotional response, such as anxiety, fear or shame (see page 127 for more on shame). The emotion drives a behavioural response that attempts to manage the distress felt. These behaviours or rituals are known as compulsions, for example, going back to check that the door is locked for a third, fourth, fifth time. After all, what's a little time compared to losing your family?

Compulsions can be overt and easy to identify, such as washing hands, touching or tapping, or covert and unseen, occurring only in our heads, such as replaying conversations or going over situations to check that you haven't caused any harm. They are behaviours that are intended to reduce emotional distress and prevent any harm that the sufferer fears they will be responsible for.

The reason why some people attach such importance and meaning to intrusive cognitions is not fully understood. It may be related to childhood experiences of being blamed or having to care for others. Genetics may also play a part. In my experience, OCD sufferers often have experiences that have led them to conclude bad things not only can happen but will happen. For them, the world can seem like a very unpredictable and unsafe place. In children, a small number of cases with a sudden onset are linked to infection. OCD sufferers are often cautious people who are highly self-critical, fear doing any harm and often feel a great deal of responsibility. They may try and plan for every eventuality and struggle with uncertainty. They are often very hard-working and sometimes perfectionists. They are very often thoughtful, sensitive people who have a strong urge to protect others. The irony being they usually come to therapy with the belief they are 'bad', or there is something fundamentally 'wrong' with them. The demands of obsessions and compulsions mean they are all too often exhausted and depressed.

The problem with these compulsions is that they are only a quick fix and soon the anxiety resurfaces, giving rise to the need for a further compulsion. In this way, compulsions actually fuel anxiety. They can begin to take up vast amounts of time, such that someone repeatedly checking the locks on doors and windows might never leave home, or someone constantly checking through their memory bank might never leave their head! The problem is that the more we check, the less certain we become.

As many parents will be reading this book, I wanted to mention perinatal OCD. This is OCD that occurs during pregnancy or during the first year or so after birth. It can happen to mothers and fathers. Common obsessions include worrying about physically harming or sexually abusing your baby or child or making a decision about care that is 'wrong' and harmful, including giving them a disease or infecting them in some way. This can be highly frightening. Common compulsions include avoiding touching your baby, avoiding spending time alone with them, excessive washing of clothes and asking for a lot of reassurance. Again, the list goes on. Remember that in OCD, the brain latches on to distressing thoughts. It results from being responsible and caring – not being bad. Please seek help from a professional who specialises in OCD and its treatment.

In 'The Shadow Monster', one day (quite randomly) something Mouse perceives as dangerous pops into his life, like an OCD sufferer might find a thought that they perceive as hazardous pops into their minds. At first, Mouse tries to push this 'monster' away, but much to his dismay, it simply gets bigger and stronger. The more he pushes, the stronger it gets. A fear that something terrible will happen starts to consume him. He believes that his friends or family might get hurt and that he will be responsible. As a result, he spends day and night trying to contain the monster. He compulsively checks that each stone in the wall is secure and each lock functions properly, working himself to the point of exhaustion to keep everyone safe. Only at the point at which the monster threatens his life does he seek help from Badger.

Badger helps Mouse to see that monsters aren't always what they seem. What we think we see might be frightening, but it isn't always true or real. More than this, Badger helps him see how irrational it is that a mouse who works so hard to keep everyone safe and worries so much about them getting hurt would be a bad mouse.

Badger's support gives Mouse the belief and courage to leap into the jaws of the monster. In facing his fear in this way, he strips it of its power. The 'monster' collapses and is revealed to be nothing but a mass of brambles that had grown through a hole in the wall.

Changing the Story: What Helps

It is possible to heal from OCD and anxiety, and here are some simple suggestions about the sort of things that might help on the road to recovery. If they don't, it's not a sign of failure. Quite often, professional help and support are needed first. It is vital to seek help from a professional when mental health difficulties are having a significant impact on life and affecting daily functioning. The guidance given here is not exhaustive and you will find plenty of information online to supplement it, as well as many valuable organisations that offer specialist help.

Learn about OCD and anxiety. Understanding and naming OCD for what it is can really help, particularly with feelings of shame. Learning about OCD can help you identify early warning signs, such as repetitive behaviours, and respond accordingly. This book is a good start but there are plenty of resources out there, many of them online.

Get help. If you are a parent or carer struggling with OCD, it is important to get help as your child will pick up on your anxieties and behaviours. Seek help from a specialist who understands OCD as it is unlikely to go away by itself and most adult sufferers can recall symptoms in their childhood. Speak to your GP. They might be able to refer you or your child to someone who can help. Support groups can be a useful resource. It's important to know you're not alone.

If you have a child struggling with OCD, there are many ways you can help:

Name it. Children with OCD need to understand the condition and that it is nothing to be ashamed of. It can be helpful to give it a name like 'the bully'. Saying things such as 'It's not you, it's your OCD' can create a sense of separation that can also be helpful.

Be kind but firm. Whilst it is important to be non-judgemental and supportive if your child is struggling with OCD, it is also important to be firm. Unsurprisingly, parents often behave in ways to try and reduce the distress they see their children experiencing. The problem is that these ways of behaving or accommodations actually reinforce worries

119

and make matters worse. Say your child has a fear of food contamination and demands that you only cook certain things in a certain way. It might seem better and easier to go along with their compulsion, but it will only validate their anxiety. The same goes for excessive reassurance. Your child is looking for a certainty that you can't give them. Set limits and be consistent. In the short term, your child may express some anger and distress, but over time this will decrease anxiety. You can say something such as 'I know that this is really difficult for you. Your OCD is making you really scared right now. It's a bully, and we have to stand up to bullies.' Getting the balance right can be difficult, though. Limits are best agreed and introduced gradually. Find professional support to help you with how to do this.

Understand how stress affects OCD. Stress is likely to make OCD worse. There will be good days and bad days. It is important to acknowledge this. You can say something such as 'You've got a maths test tomorrow, no wonder you're struggling with your OCD at the moment.' Help your child manage their stress levels by looking at the soothing strategies given in the trauma section.

Do something else. Distraction can help when feeling the urge to carry out a compulsion. Think about what form this might take, for example, listening to music, reading a book, playing with a pet, drawing, or whatever may help.

Be kind. Remember, everyone has intrusive thoughts so help your child to be kind to themselves. OCD doesn't reflect a deficit in personality. Sufferers are often caring and sensitive people who feel a great deal of responsibility.

THREE
Understanding More About Attachment

FINDING SOMEONE THERE

We are born seeking attachment to others, and our attachment style is formed in response to the quality of care we receive from caregivers in our early years of life. There are four broad categories of attachment: secure, avoidant, ambivalent and disorganised. We can have different attachment relationships with different people, and no one ever fits neatly into just one category. However, we tend to have a default position or style. This story explores avoidant attachment. Whatever your or your child's style of attachment, it is possible to change it.

When babies and children receive sufficiently warm and responsive care, they develop a secure attachment. They develop an expectation that their emotional and relational needs will be adequately met by those around them. Children with a secure attachment understand their feelings and can use them for problem-solving. They are emotionally well regulated and show good levels of self-esteem.

If, as a child, you received the sort of care that means you have developed a secure attachment style, the chances are you will automatically parent your own children in the same way. If, like many others, you weren't that fortunate, you are also likely to automatically parent your children in the same way you were parented. Even if you try to make changes, knowing certain things weren't right, you might find it challenging to find the right balance. The problem is you have only learnt how *not* to do it. Not knowing how to do something because you haven't been taught to do it shouldn't be a source of shame (see page 127 for more about shame). If you recognise something of yourself or your child in an avoidant style, remember that it is something you can change – no matter how old you or your child are.

It is also worth mentioning that some cultures, including our traditional British culture of the 'stiff upper lip' and 'big boys (and girls) don't cry', reinforce a style of parenting that can lead to an avoidant attachment style – as does the overvaluing of independence and self-reliance also endorsed by these cultures.

When carers are emotionally unresponsive or cold, when they dismiss or disapprove of a child's emotions or needs, or they are hostile towards them, children soon learn to stop expressing their emotions or even feeling them! They adapt by withdrawing emotionally and stop seeking closeness. They don't want to risk the pain of rejection that might follow. Rejection of emotion can include rejection of positive feelings such as excitement and happiness, as well as things like anger, sadness and fear.

Caregivers often want their child to be independent and stand on their own two feet. They might believe that to survive, their child needs to be strong and that focusing on negative emotions will only worsen things. They might see emotion as an indication that something needs to be fixed. Although these caregivers dismiss emotions, they can often care deeply about their children and want the very best for them.

As these children adapt through not expressing emotion or showing needs, they can often appear self-reliant and self-contained. They may even appear calm whilst experiencing high levels of hidden anxiety. There can be a sense of underlying anger and subtle non-compliance. They may seem aloof or cold, not seeking others for relationship or support, believing they shouldn't have needs. They may be withdrawn, isolated and solitary, but they may also join in – even be the life and soul – whilst finding ways of avoiding real closeness. They are likely to fear rejection and be sensitive to it. They may also be overtly angry and hostile towards others.

These individuals have, in effect, taken the vulnerable, needing, emotional part of themselves and hidden it, and then left a non-needing, non-wanting, non-emotional coping part to face the world. The vulnerable part is protected in this way. But the lack of real connection leads to a profound sense of loneliness and emptiness. They can have a sense of being unwanted or untouchable. When adults or adolescents who grew up this way come into therapy, they often express a sense of something missing without knowing what it is, along with feelings of emptiness and loneliness. As they tend to focus on tasks rather than relationships, they are often highly capable and even high performing.

The combination of fear of rejection and loneliness creates a dilemma. Coming forward to connect risks being attacked and rejected with little hope of being met with love and acceptance. Not doing so risks the continued terror of being completely alone. A compromise position can be taken, seeming to be a solution of sorts. Being neither in nor out of a relationship has many faces but might look like simply being present or engaging in a cognitive or practical, task-focused way.

In the story, Squirrel buries his vulnerable, emotional, wanting and needing part in response to a cold, hostile environment. He buries it so deep, he loses all conscious awareness of it, but he does have a sense of something missing and of there being at least the possibility of something different, something that feels warm – like the sun on the inside. It is this feeling that compels his search.

Squirrel is independent and somewhat solitary. He has a tendency to 'get on with it' and dismiss his own experience. When Hare suggests that living through a long, cold winter must have been hard, he replies that he 'got used to it'.

Although it is initially unknown to Squirrel, in order to overcome his feelings of emptiness and reconnect with the lost part of himself, Squirrel needs someone to earn the trust of this intensely vulnerable part and meet it with acceptance and empathy. To begin, he has little hope of finding this. The fear of further rejection and attack makes him move away from relationships, whilst the terror of loneliness forces him towards them.

Finding Hare is a pivotal moment in his quest. She represents an attuned, empathic, 'good-enough' other, with whom Squirrel can form a reparative relationship. She seems somewhat strange and confusing to him as she responds in unexpected ways. Early on in their relationship, Squirrel experiences a conflict. One part wants to come forward to connect and escape loneliness, whilst the other wants to move away in fear of experiencing further pain. This is represented in physical movement where Squirrel takes a 'relational' step forward and then back.

Their journey together is a long one. They encounter many things, there are conflicts and many emotions, but Squirrel never cries. He has not yet grown to trust Hare enough to let her see this most vulnerable part.

The concluding part of the journey comes when they reach the wood. This represents a step into Squirrel's past. The old oak is a fortress, a well-defended place of retreat in which Squirrel hid the vulnerable part of himself. Hare understands that his withdrawal brought safety at the cost of loneliness. She can also see it was an act of courage that symbolised something extraordinary and profound about his ability to survive a hostile environment. Finally, Squirrel feels safe enough to step fully into a connection with Hare and reveal his whole self; he asks for her help and cries. Finding his sadness met with empathy, he can move beyond his past. They leave the wood, and Squirrel discovers something new inside.

Ultimately, Squirrel's journey with Hare, a journey in which he comes to see Hare for who she truly is (a kind, trustworthy animal, rather than the frightening animal he thought she was at the beginning of the story) and finding the hidden parts of himself are inextricably linked. In finding her, he finds the trust to make connections. This trust of connection fills him with a feeling of warmth.

There is no definitive moment of change, more a series of events that eventually lead them to the place where Squirrel needs to be. Squirrel shows his understanding of this when Hare asks him where he found the thing he was looking for and he says, 'Somewhere along the way with you.'

Changing the Story: What Helps

It is possible to heal from avoidant attachment and here are some simple suggestions about the sort of things that might help the road to recovery. If they don't, it's not a sign of failure. Quite often, professional help and support are needed first. It is vital to seek help from a professional when mental health difficulties are having a significant impact on life and affecting daily functioning. The guidance given here is not exhaustive and you will find plenty of information online to supplement it, as well as many valuable organisations that offer specialist help.

If you think your child might have an avoidant attachment style, it is best to get help from a professional. There might be another explanation and you are likely to need support with managing your own feelings as you try to change things. You can look at the soothing strategies given under trauma (see page 109) to manage your stress levels.

Ask for help and show feelings. Avoidant children need help shifting from a strong focus on tasks to one that is more balanced, so that attention is not only given to activities but people and relationships too. Avoidant children often appear independent and unemotional, but this is usually because they keep their feelings hidden and think it is not okay to ask for help. They avoid contact rather than seek it when anxious. They need someone to help them understand that it is okay to ask for help and show their feelings.

Offer support. While it is good to praise children for managing tasks independently and as parents, we often take pride in our children's capabilities, they must know that they can ask for help. Think about offering support if you see them struggling to do something or ask if they would like some help even if it seems they can manage.

Empathise. See if you can think about what your child might be feeling. For example, if a friend cancels a playdate, think about the sort of feelings they might have. They might feel sad, hurt, rejected, angry or embarrassed. Then, make a suggestion such as 'I wonder if you're feeling sad because your playdate was cancelled.' Don't worry if you're wrong about the feeling. You're opening up a communication line and making it okay to talk about feelings and what causes them.

Observe and communicate. You can also help your child notice their feelings and body sensations. You might say something such as 'You seem worried today. Your body looks really tight, like you're holding yourself together.' You could also say something such as 'When I feel angry, I notice I clench my fists and my jaw, or when I get worried, my tummy hurts.' See if you can help them identify what caused the feeling. For example, you might say something such as 'I wonder if you're feeling worried because you'll be getting a different teacher today.'

Four
Understanding More About Shame

The Most Beautiful Tail

This is a story about chronic or toxic shame. Talking about shame can be tricky. Shame is a normal emotion that, when handled well by caregivers, helps keep behaviour in check, develops empathy and increases resilience. We start to feel shame in the first couple of years of life when we see disappointment or disapproval in caregivers' eyes in response to something we have done. When this look of disappointment is quickly replaced with a look of love and a repair is done, the shame we feel is bearable and healthy, helping us function well in life and society.

Chronic or toxic shame is different. It develops when shame-based interactions are overused by caregivers to manage behaviour and no repair is done. The look of disapproval or the angry outburst isn't followed by a look of love or forgiveness. Instead, the child is treated with hostility or is rejected. The child begins to develop a sense not of 'I've done something wrong' but 'I *am* something wrong'. There is a pervasive sense of 'I'm bad'. Clients frequently report a sense of 'There's something wrong with me'. If the rejection follows a child expressing a need or an emotion, the child may develop a sense that it is not safe or even it's wrong to show emotions or have needs.

Where there is trauma or neglect, there is always shame. But shame can exist in the absence of trauma and neglect. Clients in therapy or counselling often present feeling

127

confused and (further) ashamed of their struggles with life. They often feel as if there is nothing to explain these struggles. In these situations, you don't have to look very hard to find the psychological trauma of shame. As children, these clients had caregivers who repeatedly rejected them. There was no room for healthy protest. As children, they were usually very compliant – good girls and boys – who worked hard to avoid being 'bad'.

As a child, rejection can feel life-threatening (we can't survive without parents or caregivers). As such, shame is a survival response. It signals interpersonal or social danger.

So, what are the defensive responses to this danger? They fit the fight, flight, freeze, shutdown or flop pattern of all survival responses. In shame, there is often a strong urge to hide. It is better not to be seen. Part of this can be avoiding genuine relationships. Submission is central to shame, and there tends to be a desire to please that goes beyond the norm, becoming automatic compliance. But shame can attack too in the form of angry outbursts and blaming others or even attacks on the self.

Self-blame and hostility towards the self are always present. The need to not get things wrong for fear of being shamed can lead to perfectionism. Because we go into a survival response, as with trauma, it's difficult to think, and I find clients often struggle with finding words to express themselves. Add this to feelings of being worthless, vulnerable, scrutinised and found wanting and it's not surprising that shame can have such a devastating impact on people's lives.

It is essential to mention that shame can be induced in any hostile and rejecting environment, and it might not have anything to do with parenting. Bullying is a shame-based interaction and has enormous implications for society, particularly with the rise of social media. Shame can develop around gender, sexuality, culture and body image, to name but a few things.

In 'Beautiful Tail', Rat has grown up in a continually rejecting and hostile environment. Rat has done nothing but be a normal rat. But, as Crow points out, she just doesn't fit with the way humans want things to be. This is much like a child being a normal child with all their normal needs and emotions, making all the normal everyday mistakes that a child might make and being rejected because of it. Rat has little choice but to hide away to keep herself safe. She is too small to defend herself. Worse than that, if she's seen, she evokes horror and disgust. The mother screams and the girl cries simply because Rat is a rat. When she is caught by Cat, if Rat wants to avoid being eaten, she has to submit. She has to be a 'good' rat and do as she's told.

When she runs to the wood, Rat imagines the animals will see her the same way. Despite the animals' acceptance, the voice in her head keeps on telling her she is a stupid rat and this keeps the shame going. She is surprised by the animals' reactions to her, but it is only when she begins to see her strengths and take pride in her achievement of saving Little Rabbit that she starts to believe that there isn't anything wrong with her.

Changing the Story: What Helps

It is possible to heal from toxic shame and here are some simple suggestions about the sort of things that might help the road to recovery. If they don't, it's not a sign of failure. Quite often, professional help and support are needed first. It is vital to seek help from a professional when mental health difficulties are having a significant impact on life and affecting daily functioning. The guidance given here is not exhaustive and you will find plenty of information online to supplement it, as well as many valuable organisations that offer specialist help.

Bring shame into the open. Shame likes to hide, so it is essential to give it light and air. Help your child talk about shame. This book is a good place to start. It can be really helpful to talk about your own experiences of shame.

Understand shame as a survival response. Help your child to understand why they feel shame. For example, if they find it difficult to make eye contact and find the words to make conversation, explain how that has been a way of keeping themselves safe or stopping themselves from getting hurt or bullied. If you are a parent or other adult struggling with shame, acknowledge the same for yourself. You can also consider that the shame that kept you safe is no longer needed.

Challenge shame. Self-blame is the internal voice that keeps the shame going. Help your child to challenge this voice. Think of it as a bully that can be stood up to. To begin, help them to become aware of the voice. You could try keeping a journal together to help you notice any patterns and possible triggers. If they say something such as 'I'm so stupid', you could respond by saying something such as 'There's that bully voice again.' Now ask them to imagine a good friend saying those things about themself. Ask your child what they would say to their friend. Try and help them be more objective. For example, if they didn't do as well as they'd hoped in a test, are they too hard on themselves or is there something they can learn from the experience? Remind them that we all make mistakes sometimes. If they've struggled with finding words or making eye contact, for example, remind them it's their brain behaving as expected in shame.

Develop a sense of pride. Notice and talk about your child's achievements to help develop their self-esteem. Don't focus just on academic or sporting achievements. Notice when they say something kind or do something helpful, or even just what a beautiful smile they have.

Find helpful practices and strategies. Shame is a survival response, so it is similar in some ways to trauma. Help your child manage their stress by looking at the practices given in the section on trauma (see page 109). Feeling safe and relaxed will make things easier.

FIVE
Understanding More About Loss

WHISPERS

Grief is a natural response to loss. Children, like adults, experience a wide range of reactions and emotions. How we experience loss depends to an extent on the developmental stage. However, children develop at different rates and have different life experiences, so grief reactions are uniquely personal. As children grow and reach new developmental stages, their grief may re-emerge as they gain further understanding and insight. A child may, for example, have a different sense of what it means not to have a mother when they are thirteen years than they had when they were eight. This re-emergence of grief can be confusing to the adults around them.

Babies and toddlers, up until the age of around two years, will not understand death or what is happening around them. However, they do feel loss and experience distress in response to separation and change. They may search or ask for the person who has died and be very sensitive to the grief responses of the adults around them. Sometimes adults believe that if a child is or was too young to remember something, they cannot be impacted by it. That couldn't be further from the truth. Babies' and toddlers' grief will be seen in their behaviour, which might include increased distress, crying more, being difficult to soothe, having more tantrums and expressing more anger, or becoming quiet and withdrawn. There may be a disturbance to eating or sleeping routines.

Preschoolers will remember the person and will try to understand death but will struggle with the idea of permanence. They may expect the dead person to come back and find it hard to accept they won't. They may also forget and need to be reminded. Younger primary school-aged children become more curious about death but are still learning and can be easily confused. They may think it is temporary and the dead person can still feel things, worrying that they are cold, hungry or lonely. They might think they are responsible for the death somehow or believe that they might bring them back to life. They may also think thoughts such as they can go to heaven to visit someone or bring them home.

Somewhere around the ages of seven to ten years, children start to understand not only the permanence of death but also its inevitability. They may become more concerned about the safety and the possible death of others or themselves. They also start to become more aware of the adults around them and may try to hide their feelings to not worry them. They may also try to hide the loss from peers because of feelings of embarrassment and being different. Death may also be frightening or spooky, with fears about ghosts or skeletons.

Secondary school-aged children are more like adults in their responses. Developmentally, they are likely to experience intense emotions and so may also have intense grief reactions. They will be more aware of the longer-term consequences of death and have more adult concerns around things such as finances and who might carry out caring and housekeeping tasks. There may be an expectation that they will have to be more adult and get on with it. They may find it difficult to find the space to share their grief and experience loneliness. To manage their emotions, they may turn to alcohol and drugs and engage in risk-taking behaviours.

Common grief reactions across these age groups include:

- sleep disturbances, including problems getting to sleep and nightmares
- changes in appetite
- becoming more angry or aggressive, or more withdrawn and shut down
- mood swings, becoming more nervous or jumpy, searching or looking for the dead person

- regressive behaviours – for example, thumb-sucking, bedwetting or soiling
- increased fear of death
- physical ailments, such as headaches and tummy aches

Problems with school can begin to occur, children's grades may drop as they struggle to concentrate, or attendance may suffer as they worry about family members at home. Alternatively, they may throw themselves into their work, avoiding feeling by focusing on tasks.

Denial is a common reaction and can be seen as a coping strategy, albeit one that happens outside of conscious awareness. As a rule, children have an increased tendency to dip quickly in and out of grief, as they can only manage powerful emotions for short periods. The changes can be so quick it has been called 'puddle-jumping'. They jump in and out of puddles of grief. It might look like they don't care as they rush off to play, but that is not the case. Numbness (feeling nothing) can result from shock or delaying grief to manage the demands of life, for example, school exams. Children may also try to protect those around them from their grief and hide their feelings.

To some extent, reactions occur because children struggle to express or make sense of their feelings in other ways, such as through talking. It is important to help children understand their emotions and express them.

There is no right or wrong way to grieve. A wide range of emotions is experienced, in no particular order, over no set time. It really is a case of 'however you feel, it's okay'. Along with the feelings that we might typically expect, like sadness, it is common to experience anger, irritability, fear, anxiety, guilt, shock, numbness, depression, hopelessness and confusion.

When someone close to you has died, it is common to fear that someone else might die or to have fears about your own health. There is a sense that the world is an unreliable place where things can and do go wrong. Life feels more fragile, and children might become anxious about leaving family members alone for fear of what might happen to them in their absence.

Guilt is another typical response, perhaps even more so in children. They have a tendency to blame themselves for things that happen in their worlds, so they may consider they have been responsible in some way. It might be something practical like not having seen a parent was ill, for example, or it could be something less direct like having wished someone was dead, or simply a vague sense that had they been better in some way, it might not have happened. They may also feel guilty for being alive and particularly for experiencing enjoyment or having fun.

Mixed feelings create confusion, which can be acute if there was a strained or difficult relationship with the person that died. It can be very difficult to manage feelings of hatred or anger towards someone who has died, particularly when combined with feelings of love and sadness. This is also true of the feeling of relief that can often accompany death, particularly following an extended illness. Withholding information about death can also cause confusion and anger. If you don't give children enough information, they will fill the blanks themselves – often with painful consequences.

Anger is common for many reasons. It might be directed at the person that has died for abandoning them or not having looked after themselves, for example. They might be angry at someone for not doing more or angry at themselves for the same reason. Children can become angry if they feel they have been left out of or not consulted about funeral arrangements. This might be not being allowed to attend a funeral, see a body or not being involved in the planning of ceremonies. This sort of exclusion can often be well meaning but is usually unhelpful.

Fox's story is one of loss and grief. She feels a mixture of emotions. Guilt and regret are central to this. She feels she should have been there for Stag because he had always been there for her. She is also angry with herself for making the decision to stop and help Baby Rabbit. Though, as Crow says, she had little choice. She is perhaps also angry with Stag that he didn't wait for her a little longer. Her return to the stone wall where she first met Stag is typical behaviour in grief. A part of her may feel closer to him there. With Crow's help, Fox comes to understand that she can still find Stag in her heart and her memories. The overall theme is that our attachments or bonds continue even when someone is no longer with us.

Changing the Story: What Helps

It is possible to heal from loss and here are some simple suggestions about the sort of things that might help the road to recovery. If they don't, it's not a sign of failure. Sometimes professional help and support are needed first. It is vital to seek help from a professional when mental health difficulties are having a significant impact on life and affecting daily functioning. The guidance given here is not exhaustive and you will find plenty of information online to supplement it, as well as many valuable organisations that offer specialist help.

Be honest and factual. Answer questions honestly about the facts surrounding a death. It can be tempting to spare the truth to protect children, but this is misguided. It creates confusion and children will fill in the blanks. If it's complicated, try and anticipate the questions and work out simple, concise answers that will be understood.

Avoid using euphemisms about death. This means to avoid saying things like 'passed away', 'passed on', 'gone for a long sleep', 'gone to a better place' or 'lost'. Again, this creates confusion. A child who is told someone has gone to a 'better place' might well imagine it's better because they are not there. Or they may wonder if they might come back if they're really good or about joining them in this 'better place'. The idea of a 'long sleep' can be confusing and frightening as sleep is part of our everyday lives. Someone who is 'lost' might experience distress and potentially be found.

Help your child to understand death and loss. This is an important conversation for all children, not just for those having experienced a loss. It can be helpful to use examples from nature like a dead leaf or insect. It is important to explain that when things are dead, they can't come back. Children need to know that when someone dies, their body stops working and they can't eat, breathe or feel emotions or bodily sensations, such as pain or cold. Loss is an everyday and inevitable part of life. Friends move schools, parents break up, toys go missing, the list goes on. Children often talk to me about computer games in which characters are killed or kingdoms destroyed. All of these situations provide an opportunity for feelings to be explored and validated in a way that can help children manage and understand loss.

Reassure. Let your child know that whatever they feel, it's okay and that there is no right or wrong way to feel when you grieve. Encourage them to express their feelings. They can be helped to do this by you not being afraid to show your own feelings. Help them name and understand emotions. You might say something such as 'I'm crying because I miss Grandma and feel sad,' or 'No wonder you're upset, you wanted Grandad to be here for your birthday and he isn't.'

No blame. Your child might need a lot of reassurance that death is not their fault. They might, for example, believe that if they had a bad thought about someone, it might have brought their death about. Reassure them that it is normal to feel guilty and that it is not their fault. If relevant, explain that we can't make things happen by thinking about them and everyone has thoughts like that.

Have fun. Reassure your child that it's okay to have fun and enjoy themselves and encourage them to participate in activities they enjoy. I think it can be helpful to talk about parts – to say a part of you can go out and have fun and enjoy yourself, even though another part feels really sad.

Maintain routines. Children feel safer when routines are in place, so stick to them as much as possible.

Stay close. After a death, stay as close as possible to your child. Further separation is likely to cause anxiety. It's not a good time to book a weekend away or lots of evenings with a babysitter. Give lots of comfort in the way of hugs and cuddles.

Inclusion. Include children as much as possible in funeral arrangements. Give them all the information they need to decide if they want to be involved in rituals such as funerals and viewing the body.

Feel connected. Help children continue to feel connected to someone who has died. Talk about the person, telling stories about them. Encourage your child to tell their story as it is an important part of the grieving process. Acknowledge anniversaries in a way that feels right for you. It could be anything from visiting a grave to watching a film you all loved. When it seems hard to find the time to talk, setting a 'talk time' can be helpful. Help your child make a memory box filled with things that will remind them of the person and the times spent with them. It can include photographs and keepsakes that might prompt different memories and emotions, for example, things that might make them laugh and things that might make them cry.

Take time to heal. Adjustment to loss can take a long time. Remind children that the pain will lessen over time and it will be okay.

Next Steps

The mental health difficulties explored in this book reflect some of the most common presenting problems that I come across in my clinical practice. There is often great relief when clients discover that what pains them is both nameable and knowable. However, understanding on its own is never enough. Only when we make an emotional connection with the wounded parts of ourselves can we really start to heal. As a parent or carer, you have a vital role in helping your child do this through meaningful conversation and by being curious about and accepting of their thoughts, feelings and experience of life. Hopefully, this book can help facilitate that process.

Based largely on my personal working knowledge and clinical experience, this book can only give a general overview of the mental health problems explored. It is not an exhaustive resource. However, if you recognise something of yourself or a child in them, there are many places you can go to get further information and support. I have listed a few resources:

Childline (children and young people only)
www.childline.org.uk
0800 1111 (UK)
Available 24 hours a day for children and young people, with help and advice about a wide range of issues, the ability to talk to a counsellor online, send Childline an email or post on the message boards.

Children and Families

www.camhs-resources.co.uk

SHOUT Crisis

Text line 85258 or visit www.crisistextline.co.uk

Samaritans (for young people and adults)

www.samaritans.org

116 123 (UK), 24 hours a day

Email: jo@samaritans.org

Available 24 hours a day to provide confidential emotional support for people experiencing feelings of distress, despair or suicidal thoughts.

Young Minds

www.youngminds.org.uk

YoungMinds is the UK's leading charity committed to improving the emotional wellbeing and mental health of children and young people.

The Mix

www.themix.org.uk

Honest information and support for young people in the UK on a range of issues.

MindEd

www.minded.org.uk

At its heart, MindEd provides practical knowledge that gives adults the confidence to identify a mental health issue and act swiftly, meaning better outcomes for the child or young person involved.

NHS mental health services

Find local mental health services on the NHS website.

You can also get advice from NHS 111 phone service.

Acknowledgements

Arriving at the point at which I felt I could write this book is inextricably linked to my life journey. The animals within it are on their own journeys, searching for something they can only find with the help of the characters they meet. Characters who become not only fellow travellers and friends, but guides and conduits of change, taking them to new places of understanding and knowing.

Below are a few of my fellow travellers, some lifelong, others who joined me only recently, but all of whom have been an important part of my journey and my search. My heartfelt thanks, I am indebted to you.

To the many clients I have known and had the privilege to work with, your courageous hearts inspired these stories.

Graham Music, you so readily agreed to write the foreword for this book and gave of your time and encouragement so generously. It means more than you know. Jessica Leafe, editor extraordinaire, you have been brilliant. Di Gammage, your insightful critique was invaluable. Jo Panton, your suggestions were genius and shaped the book so much for the better. Ed Panton, you were the first to test-drive the stories, which you did with a willingness and zest that was a delight. Tor Allen, your illustrations are beautiful and brought my visions to life. Sarah Stansfield and Chandra Kantha, you offered your support so willingly.

Cath Hollin, you cried and perhaps that is one of the reasons you are my oldest friend. Alysia Mayo, your enthusiasm lifted my spirits and, as if that's not enough, you remember the duckling. Ashley Grainger, your earnest reflections touched me almost as much as the tea and cornflakes. Dad, you're no longer here, but you gave me a love of learning, and I hope you would have been proud ... and finally, to my husband, Peter and my sons, Conor and Callum.

Peter and Callum, over lockdown you became a captive audience and had little choice but to endure me reading many versions of the same stories with only minor alterations, which you did with endless patience and unwavering conviction. Whilst, Conor, despite distance, you found a way to support me through your considered comments and by giving me one of the most profound pieces of advice I have ever received, to back myself. But my thanks to you are for much more than that: they are for being my everything. Quite simply, without you and your somewhat unfathomable love, there would be no book. In fact, there would be nothing at all.

About the Author

Hayley Graham is a psychotherapist working with children, adolescents and adults. She is registered and accredited by the UKCP as a specialist child and adolescent psychotherapist, as well as being an accredited registered member of the BACP and an EMDR therapist. She has many years of experience working with children, young people and adults – both within school settings and in private practice. Hayley is the founder and director of BOUNCE! Brighter Futures Foundation, a registered charity based in Devon. BOUNCE! provides counselling and psychotherapy services for children, young people and their families, as well as providing training and support for educators. The service is delivered within primary and secondary schools, alongside low-cost therapy provision delivered directly to the community.

To anyone who is, or ever has been, a child ...
especially Mum, who had all the courage of little Fox but never
found her Stag. – HG

First published in Great Britain in 2022
by Little Steps Publishing
Vicarage House, 58-60 Kensington Church Street
London W8 4DB
www.littlestepspublishing.co.uk

ISBN: 978-1-912678-75-4

A CIP catalogue record for this book is available from the British Library.

Designed by Celeste Hulme

Printed in China
1 3 5 7 9 10 8 6 4 2